Beyond My Worth

BEYOND

MY

WORTH

BY LILLIAN ROTH

AUTHOR OF *I'll Cry Tomorrow*

NEW YORK, FREDERICK FELL, INC., PUBLISHERS

©

COPYRIGHT 1958 BY LILLIAN ROTH

Manufactured in the United States of America by H. Wolff, New York

DESIGNED BY SIDNEY SOLOMON

Published simultaneously in Canada by George J. McLeod, Ltd., Toronto

L. C. CATALOG CARD NO. 58-8740

*My gratitude to Floyd Miller for his assistance
and to the many unknown hearts I know so well*

To my husband, T. Burt McGuire, Jr.,
who has given me a love beyond my worth

Contents

Preface

This book is your book. A continuation of the Lillian Roth story is possible only because of the great contributions you have made to it.

Each step up has been with the aid of your hands, and the desire to climb yet another stems from the strength borrowed from your hearts. You have encouraged me and rewarded me with a credit beyond my worth.

When I wrote my autobiography, *I'll Cry Tomorrow*, I told frankly and honestly of my sixteen years of alcoholism and of my first, faltering steps toward sobriety and the beginning of a new life. I wrote the book with the hope that the revelation of truth would clear the cobwebs of my thinking and put things into their proper perspective. By being able to look at my life objectively, without tears or self-pity, I could perhaps also help someone else who had lost the way.

When I finished the book, I laid down my pen for good, I thought. I was not a professional writer, after all, and henceforth would concentrate on rebuilding my career as an actress and night-club entertainer. Yet here I am, five years later, writing another book. And again I am anxious to share with you the amazement of my life.

Nothing in my wildest imaginings could have prepared me for what has happened these past five years. I am not only referring to success in my theatrical career, but to the great outpouring of love and help I have received from thousands of people all over the country. And I have been sustained most by the very people who turned to me for help.

God sends us strength and understanding in strange and wonderful ways. I have received them from a psychotic in a mental hospital in Texas, a girl wasting with multiple sclerosis in Detroit, a murderer in prison in California, a priest in a primitive little parish in the wilds of Brazil. I have been allowed to see the human heart in a way seldom revealed.

These people turned to me for help, not realizing that I too suffered human frailty. But wondrously, they brought me their strength along with their fears. Through the past few years we have helped each other, and if there is to be gratitude, the greater is mine. I have survived, I have grown stronger due to the people who came to me to receive help but ended by giving it.

I have indeed cast my bread upon the waters.

1

The Arrows Still Fly

The Ninety-first Psalm says, "Thou shalt not be afraid of the terror by night, nor for the arrow that flieth by day."

The Psalm does not say there are no terrors, it only directs us to be brave in the face of them. Oh, how difficult! No matter how often we seem to be able to make our way out of the shadowed valley, no matter how often we surmount a difficulty, there are always new trials ahead to test our strength.

I've been in some mighty dark valleys. I became an alcoholic when I was in my early twenties; lost a career and movie stardom; lost my friends, security, integrity, almost my very life while I drank two quarts of whiskey a day. I have fought my way out of that valley and today I have once again material security, I have made spiritual progress, and I have the love of a fine man, my husband . . . yet I find that the arrows still fly.

[*13*]

This is true, I think, because our old weaknesses are always with us. We may have suppressed them, supplanted them with strengths, but they always lurk deep within us, awaiting a chance to surface.

I've had mornings recently when I woke up and my whole life seemed in chaos and I said to myself, "I've fallen back, I've fallen way back again." I don't mean in the problem of alcoholism, for I know when I keep God in mind I'll keep my problem in hand. But old weaknesses, my erratic tendencies, my melancholia were coming to the surface again. I'd snap at my husband, Burt, be dissatisfied with life in general, not want to see people for a week at a time. Those who came in contact with me would think, "Well, there's the same old Roth, acting up again. She's impossible."

I was in New York during one of these depressed periods recently, sitting in my hotel room and staring out the window at the canyons and cliffs of Manhattan. It was late afternoon, and as the purple twilight settled about the skyscrapers a million lights flicked on and it became a jeweled city. I had only to reach out my hand for it, but it seemed to hold nothing for me. I was tired and discouraged and the simplest problem of living seemed insurmountable.

Suddenly the room was intolerably small. I began to get the dry jitters. The walls actually seemed to be moving in on me, smothering me. Palpitations shook me and I couldn't get my breath, couldn't swallow. My skin began to itch and crawl. Panic was rising in me. I fought it, try-

ing to remember the old remedies. Calm . . . calm . . .
breathe deeply and slowly . . . get outdoors in the fresh
air. I grabbed my coat and rushed out and began walking
down Fifth Avenue. St. Patrick's Cathedral loomed up before me and I walked up the steps. Just inside the church, I
accidentally jostled a gray-haired, well-dressed man and for
a brief moment we looked at each other. Even in my dis-
traut condition I recognized that he too had come here with
a problem. There was pain and bewilderment in his eyes.
He nodded briefly in apology and walked down the center
aisle, his shoulders slumped. I found an empty pew and sank
down wearily. I closed my eyes and tried to talk to God.
I said, "God, something is terribly wrong. I don't know
what it is, I don't know how to correct it. I've tried hard
to overcome my ingratitude, my intolerance and temper.
But I just feel lost and unworthy. I don't know what else
to say except I hope You'll give me some sign to let me
know what to do, to let me know things will be all right."

This sounds rather childish, I guess, yet I didn't know
what else to do. Certainly, I didn't believe that God was
going to come down and perform some sort of miracle for
me, I didn't believe that His sole occupation was concern
for my own little problems, but I needed Him.

After my little plea I opened my eyes and sat there
quietly for a time. A few rows in front of me, a man suddenly got up and started his way back toward the exit. I
recognized him as the same gentleman I had encountered
when I entered the church. But a change had come over

him. His shoulders were straight, his step firm, and his eyes no longer seemed troubled. He paused when he reached my pew and looked calmly into my eyes. Then he smiled and said to me: "God loves you."

As he disappeared through the exit I knew that he had come to find peace and courage, that he had found it, and that he wanted me to know.

After he was gone, a feeling of peace flooded through me. Not all my problems were solved, of course, but I now knew there was a solution. God loves me, I thought, and that is my strength. I had known it all along, but somehow I had forgotten it for the moment. It took a stranger to remind me.

Walking back up Fifth Avenue toward my hotel I took inventory of myself, wondering what made me so frequently self-centered and forgetful of God's love. I had been thinking of my weaknesses and failures instead of the positive things of my life.

I, of all people, should be ever mindful of God's goodness and His concern. There have been two very difficult periods in my life, and I could not have survived either without His help. The first one was my period of alcoholism, and I've already written of that in *I'll Cry Tomorrow*. The second, which was almost as difficult but in an entirely different way, came during these past five years, after my rehabilitation and along with my new success. In the first period I had somehow to summon the energy to save myself, to save a single human being; in the second period I felt for a time that I was being asked to save half the world. How wrong I was! Who was I to think I could do more than the next person? But I went on creating tasks and problems for myself. It was a dark journey.

The second period began with the publication of my book, in June, 1954. I was playing the Anniversary Show at the Palace Theater in New York at the time and the audiences were so good to me. What pleased me most was that at least half of each audience was comprised of teen-agers, and it was great fun when they crowded the stage entrance to wait for autographs at the end of each performance. It was like old times. Mothers and fathers came to hear the old songs, the kids came to hear the new ones, and I was so pleased that I was able to bridge the generations.

The publication date of *I'll Cry Tomorrow* was on a Thursday, as I remember it, and I was most apprehensive about its reception. My life was between the covers of that book and I felt quite naked and vulnerable before the eyes of the critics and the reading public. I had held back nothing of myself and after I once got it down on paper, I was never able to reread it. I didn't read the galley proofs, nor have I ever read the book from beginning to end. I tried it several times, but it was too painful to relive those years. As publication day approached, I also was afraid that I had gone too far in self-revelation. The public had forgiven me and welcomed me back, but now when they read the whole truth about me, they might not like me and I might lose everything again.

I felt very reticent about the book, and the thought that a critic might rip into it, perhaps call it vulgar or sensational, made me curl up inside. It was an honest book and I prayed it would be looked at in that light.

My fears were unfounded. The critics were generous with approval and so was almost everybody else. The book became a best seller almost overnight. The book was placed on sale in the lobby of the Palace and now the people at the stage door besieged me for autographs on the flyleaf of *I'll Cry Tomorrow*. Soon I was flooded with offers of theater, hotel, night club, and TV bookings. Hollywood started bidding for my life's story, and the book was translated into eighteen languages, including a special edition in Braille.

During those first weeks it all seemed just too fantastically wonderful to be really true. Often, when I'd finally get to bed in the small hours of the morning, I'd say to myself, "Lillian, in many ways you're the same girl you were ten years ago. Can this really have happened to you? Can you have come so far, or is it all a dream? Which is the reality, the nightmare of alcoholism or this fantasy of success and adulation?" The years separating the two extremes seemed to shrink to nothing. The emotional response to sudden and overwhelming success can be as intoxicating as alcohol.

But it was real, all right. Part of what made it real to me were the frightening responsibilities that came with my success. I had written the book in the hope it would help others, but I wasn't prepared for the deluge that was to sweep over me following its publication. Thousands of people wrote me, and hundreds came to me in person for help, all of them thinking that I had some secret, some magic pill for overcoming illness and defeat. Some of them, much to my embarrassment, even thought that by seeing me or touching me they would be helped.

The truth was that I had no secret. I had perseverance born of desperation. But if I could not help these people, neither could I turn them away.

Each time I was exposed to the ache of another human being I took some of it on myself. I couldn't help it. I was not a professional psychiatrist or a priest. I was an ordinary woman with nothing to shield me from their hurts. It seemed a paradox that I, the weak one, should be called upon. I projected myself into the other person and empathized with them. I had long been doing this with alcoholics, of course, but now I began to do it with others as well. I'd talk to people ill with disease and feel their pains in my body; I'd talk to mentally disturbed people and feel a haziness or a spinning in my own head; and I'd talk to the lonely and feel deserted and frightened.

I was they, and they were me, so what could I say? How could I help? We were only weakness compounded.

At night I would go on the stage to sing and dance, and

people would applaud and say, "How gay and happy you are. You love what you're doing." And I did love it, but with an ache. I knew that all those people out there in the audience were happy for a moment, but that shadows lay waiting for them. I could make them forget their problems for a short time, but that wasn't enough. They expected me to help them, but all I could do was hurt with them.

My mail became an avalanche and I spent long hours every day reading and answering it.

After a time I began to worry what this was doing to me. You can't go around carrying the weight of part of the world on your shoulders. If I kept this up something was bound to give. I began to detect signs of approaching physical and emotional exhaustion. It finally came.

It was a few months after my book had been published and the pleas for help were increasing daily. I was playing in the Bradford Hotel in Boston, my home town, and I had had a particularly strenuous time with many interviews and radio and TV appearances. On the second day I was alone in my room just prior to show time. Standing before the dressing-table mirror, I began to apply my make-up when suddenly everything went dark. My eyes were open, but there was only darkness. There was no spinning in my head, no nausea, just blackness . . . blindness!

Panic exploded inside me and my mind raced crazily back . . . back to the darkness that overtook me at the age of five—a case of temporary blindness caused by the strong

Klieg lights in the motion picture studio . . . back twelve years, when I had committed myself into Bloomingdale Hospital as an alcoholic. They had examined me and I remember the doctor's slow, measured words: "Lillian, if you don't stop drinking you'll go blind. Even now I'm not certain we can save your sight. You've damaged a lot of nerve tissue, but if you stop now, forever, you've got a chance."

I had stopped! I hadn't had a drink for twelve years!

This wasn't the madhouse, this was Boston. And I was sober, and making a comeback! This couldn't be happening to me, but it was.

I felt screams building beneath the panic, threatening to cut through the smothering, the gagging. I gripped the dressing table hard, with all my strength, and I said to myself, wait, come to a dead stop. Then I began most slowly a Hail Mary, getting one painful word out at a time.

"Hail . . . Mary . . . full . . . of . . . grace, the Lord is with Thee. Blessed art Thou among women and blessed is the fruit of Thy womb, Jesus. Holy Mary, Mother of God, pray for us sinners now and at the hour of our death. Amen."

By the time the prayer was ended my vision had returned.

I had several of these spells that week, and I have never been entirely free from them to this moment. Yet I didn't go to a doctor. This was my particular problem—just between God and myself. I felt there was little a doctor could do. I don't like to pamper myself physically, and only see a physician when it's absolutely necessary. I remember the story in the newspapers about a ninety-eight-year-old preacher who was run down and killed while crossing the street in a Mid-Western town. He had never been to a doctor in his whole life, had never had an ache or a pain, yet when they performed an autopsy on him they found just about everything wrong. He had gallstones, heart trouble, a diseased liver, but he never knew it. He was one with God and so he never realized he was sick.

My moments of blindness now came quite frequently and without warning. I had to learn to live with them, and to conceal them from the public. If I was talking to someone when it happened, I'd simulate a cough, giving myself an excuse to turn away and say my little prayer and wait for sight to return.

I've had to smile to myself at times when I've overheard people say, "Did you see that expression come over her face a moment ago? And she didn't even answer my question. She's a strange one, all right."

Whenever the blindness came during my act, I'd stop right in the middle of the song and laugh and say, "I don't think that song fits our mood." I would start to tell some humorous little story while praying mentally until my vision was normal again.

I thought I was doing a pretty good job of concealing my problem. But one night, after a show, Burt said to me, "It happened again tonight, didn't it?"

"You knew?"

He nodded. "All along. I've been praying for you."

Burt and I discussed it and we both decided it was due to nerves, and the nerves due to the pressures I was feeling because of all the demands on my time. Having diagnosed it to our satisfaction, we stopped talking about it. We try never to dwell on unpleasant things. But we continued to pray that our strength would be replenished so that we might give of it to others.

Then one night, when I began to pray to God for special endurance and wisdom, I stopped and thought to myself that this was all wrong. I was asking God to make me His special deputy, to give me some of His strength so I could pass it out here on earth. What presumption on my part! What ego to think that I should be chosen to help Him do His work. And the truth was, I didn't want to play God's little angel. I only wanted His help in facing something that seemed to overwhelm me. And, quite truthfully, I was becoming a little resentful of the role I had been cast in. I didn't want to live in a glass house. I began to get rather bitter about it, I'm afraid. But what could I do?

I left Boston for a club in Toronto, Canada. Before the supper show on the first evening there was a knock at my door and I opened it to find a sweet-faced, middle-aged woman standing there and clasping a copy of my book to her bosom. When she saw me, tears flooded her eyes and she was unable to speak. I took her by the hand and led

her into my room, noticing that she walked with a very
stiff and jerky gait, as if there was something wrong with
her spine.

She soon poured out her story. She was a registered
nurse and though alone in the world had been able to
lead a fairly happy and secure life until about five years
ago. She had slipped and as a result her entire cranial,
spinal, and pelvic structure was locked in place. She had
been to doctors all over the country until her funds were
exhausted. She had taken long and expensive treatments
from osteopathic surgeons, but with no improvement,
and now she was absolutely destitute. She was without a
single relative, a single person in the whole world to
love or care for her.

When she finished her story she sat in silence for a
moment. I reached over and took her hand in mine.
"What am I to do?" she asked. "I can't work any longer.
The doctors can't seem to help me. All that's ahead is
public charity, living out my life as an invalid on a cot in
the poorhouse. I can't be so useless. I can't."

Tears came to her eyes, and to mine, too. We sat in
silence, in pain and bafflement.

"When I read your book," she said, "it was such a comfort to me. You were so strong and brave."

Strong and brave? I was certainly neither at this moment. My heart ached for this woman. And what could I
do for her? Oh God . . . what?

At this moment, Burt came into the room and motioned to his watch that it was time for the show. I went on stage and sang, "It's a Wonderful World," as if there was nothing but happiness surrounding us.

After the supper show, I went back to my hotel room to rest a few hours before the midnight show. Only there was no rest for me this time. Because of my erratic hours of work, complicated by rehearsals, press interviews, and a constant stream of visitors, it was often difficult for the maids to bring any order into my rooms until late in the evening. This particular evening, the maid was still there when I returned.

I saw that the rooms were neat, she had finished her work, yet she remained to perform little chores, straightening the blinds, fluffing the pillows on the sofa, flicking imaginary bits of dust from the window sill. I recognized the symptoms. She wanted to talk to me but hadn't yet worked up the courage. And before she could do so she burst into tears. Putting my arm around her shoulders, I led her to the sofa and we sat down together to wait for her convulsive sobs to subside enough to let her talk.

She was a woman of forty-five, but old beyond her years with work-roughened hands and lank gray hair that probably had never known the luxury of a beauty shop. She was certainly a woman accustomed to hard work, but not to the degree of heartbreak she now suffered.

"Oh the disgrace . . . the disgrace . . . it's terrible . . . terrible," she said over and over in a broken, choked voice.

"What is it? What's so terrible? So disgraceful? What's happened?"

"I've done everything a mother could. I raised her in the Church, a God-fearing, Catholic girl . . . and now this!" A new storm of sobs shook her. Finally she turned her red, swollen face to me and said, "My daughter is not married and she's pregnant. Oh Miss Roth, what am I going to do? How can I stand it?"

A frightened pregnant girl, a mother with a broken heart —in all of time how often had this tragedy struck a home? How often had sin and remorse become overwhelming? But the knowledge alone would not help this woman. That others had suffered through it would be of no comfort to her. Yet, she would survive, just as the others had. Was there any comfort in knowing that she would go on living? Perhaps not. What could I say to her?

Finally, I said, "One thing I'm certain of, you should continue to love your daughter. Now, more than ever, she needs your love."

"But the disgrace," she wailed. "How could she do such a thing?"

"My dear, before God created the Church he made Adam and Eve, and you know they sinned. We all have inherited some of that. In your daughter the flesh won over the spirit for the moment, but that doesn't mean she's a bad girl. That's what we have the confessional for in the Church, to ask God's forgiveness, and to start anew."

"But she wants to keep the baby," she cried. "It should go to an orphanage but she wants to keep it."

"She's a mother, whether married or not, and she'll love her baby. And certainly it's not the baby's fault. Why should an infant suffer the sins of the parent?"

"What will the neighbors think? Oh, it will be terrible."

"This is a problem between your daughter and God. The neighbors have nothing to do with it."

She took her face between her hands and stared at the floor with a dull, defeated gaze. What ever I had said, whether wise or unwise, had failed to give her comfort. She murmured, "She's ruined her life, ruined it. And mine, too."

I felt a surge of anger, and somehow I welcomed it because it freed me of too great a feeling of responsibility for this woman. I said, rather crossly, "Her life is not necessarily ruined. At the moment it seems to her, and to you, that it is pretty well smashed up, but it can be put back together again, with God's help. He knows we are weak and often sinful, but also that we *want* to be better and He is ready at all times to forgive, to help us start over. And once He has forgiven, what does it matter that the neighbors may gossip?"

But the woman continued to shake her head sadly, uncomprehendingly. I said, more softly, "She'll get married one day and all this will be nothing but a bad memory.

[27]

There will come along a boy who will understand, who will love her and marry her. You and your daughter must believe that."

Finally, she heaved herself erect and left the room, her shoulders drooping with an insupportable burden. I lay down to rest up for the midnight show. Rest? With the vision of a frightened young girl and a broken mother before me, there was little rest.

2

We Must Find the Way

It seems to me that sometimes the good Lord holds Himself back from helping us too soon or too often because He doesn't want us to turn to Him for the solution to every problem. I think He looks at us and says to Himself, "Well, now, the answer to her problem is right there in front of her. How much better if she can find it all on her own than if I point it out to her. She's suffering a little bit right now, but it will strengthen her for what's to come."

Certainly I know that in my own life, when things become almost insupportable and I think I just can't take it any longer, I find the solution, the way out. The answer is there. It had always been there, but I had been too busy feeling sorry for myself to work it out. I think God gives us the tools, then he waits to see how we use them.

I didn't understand this all at once, of course. It was a

gradual revelation, and at first sparked by a girl named Jean Thoney. She was a thirty-seven-year-old woman who had been in a wheel chair for almost twenty years with multiple sclerosis. Each year, each month, she wasted away a bit more, but she had an unquenchable spirit. More than that, she had a delicious sense of humor about herself. She had found the tools God had given her. We entered into correspondence and I found myself looking forward each week to her letters.

Here was a paralyzed and dying girl helping *me!* And all unbeknownst to her. As I thought about it, I realized how much help there was available to me from everyone I met. The woman with cranial lock had said to me, "I can't be so useless . . . I can't!" But I had misunderstood her. She wanted to continue to be a nurse, to serve others, and she had too much pride for charity. That was not false pride, it was a feeling of self-worthiness. Instead of breaking my heart over her, I should have admired her courage and even tried to borrow some of it for myself.

One by one I reviewed the people who had asked me for help, the ones I thought had depressed me so, and invariably they had brought with them a light, however small and flickering, an unquenchable burning of the human spirit. They were often unaware that they had the fire within them, but it was there. And it was something, selfish though it may sound, by which I could warm myself.

There were some, like Jean Thoney, who bore such a

wondrous flame that I was more than warmed by it—I was inspired, lifted completely out of myself. By all ordinary measurements Jean's life was tragic to the extreme, yet she surmounted it all and achieved a serenity of spirit that few of us can hope for. Perhaps she had to endure the pain, walk through the shadowed valley, in order to achieve the summit—I don't know. The great author, Henry James, wrote, "our very infirmities help us unexpectedly."

Jean was twenty years old when the disease struck her, in October, 1937. Twenty years old! What a magic age for most girls, on the threshold of life. For Jean it was the threshold of death. She was living in her home town of Marquette, Michigan, and working in a bakery. Here's what happened, in her own words.

"Usually the first multiple sclerosis symptoms are in the eyes, double vision and such, but with me the tips of my fingers got numb. I complained about it for a week and the family thought it was because I worked with cellophane at the bakery, which made sense to me, and when the symptom disappeared I thought no more about it. Then, on a Monday morning, my feet were both asleep, you know that prickly sensation, and I kept banging them against the bakery counter to try and wake them up. During the next few days the prickly sensation began to climb up my legs and by the end of the week it would race up to my knees. Whenever that happened I'd just fall down.

"Friday I staggered to work. I was cranky, hadn't slept well. At the end of work I wrapped up my dirty uniforms and set out for home, taking a short-cut through the cemetery. There was a hill there, but I thought I could make it. Now, I think most kids have something in their childhood that has scared them, for me it was dead people. Whenever there was a funeral in our neighborhood I would be terrified and I would stay with my grandmother until it was over. So that trip through the cemetery was going to be a tough one, I knew, but I thought I could make it.

"The prickles were half-way up to my knees when I entered the cemetery and I hurried, staggeringly, desperate to make the hill and be free of the dead. I had gone about a hundred yards when I felt my knees begin to give way. I grasped a tombstone and slumped against it. It was marble and cold as death itself and it sent a shiver through me . . . but I could not let go. I didn't want to spend the night in the cemetery alone and I was half bawling, half laughing at myself and saying over and over, 'This is ridiculous . . . this is ridiculous.'

"Fear can do wonderful things, I guess. I managed to pull myself erect, stiffen my legs, and teeter on out of that cemetery. I fell several times on the way home, but I got home. I didn't spend that night with the dead.

"The family was very concerned about me and Gram, who was living with us then, took off my dirty clothes and then insisted I bathe my feet in hot water, put some liniment on my legs, eat a good supper and go to bed. You know, we Irish have the philosophy that nothing is as bad as it appears and a full stomach plus a good night's sleep will do wonders. So all my family, Mom and Dad and my sister and Gram and I, tried to be cheerful and dig into a fragrant supper of stew. When Gram sat down on her chair, however, it rocked unevenly.

" 'What in the world is under this chair? It won't set level,' she complained, squirming on the seat, rocking it back and forth.

"She and I looked down to see what was wrong and discovered one leg of her chair was resting on the instep of my left foot. I hadn't felt a thing. This marked the end of my family's Irish optimism and before the week was out the local doctors had given up on me and I was on my way, on a stretcher in a baggage car, to the University Hospital in Ann Arbor, Michigan."

When Jean arrived at the hospital, her disease was diagnosed as multiple sclerosis. This meant that she was doomed to a long, slow, declining invalidism while her muscles wasted away. In her particular case the disease struck at her intestines and kidneys and the doctors at once surrounded her poor body with a variety of apparatus; a portable chest respirator, catheters for both her bladder and intestines, and all sorts of intravenous injection needles and tubes and bottles.

And how did Jean react to all this? Like any twenty-year-old caught in helplessness and terror; she wept for hours on end, she became resentful, and full of self-pity. She was so uncooperative with the medical staff that the doctors sent for her mother, who made the five-hundred-mile trip to see her.

Jean's description of her mother's visit reveals a good deal about that remarkable woman.

"Most mothers, I should imagine, would walk into a room, see their child in such a terrible condition, and burst into tears. But there were no tears for my Mom. She was all business when she sat down beside my bed.

" 'We've got to have a little talk,' she said. 'They've diagnosed your case and you're going to be here for a long time. Everyone here wants to help you and if you're nice to them, they'll be nice to you and everyone's life will be a lot easier. I don't want any more bad reports about you, about your not eating and not cooperating with the doctors and nurses. I've got a job I've got to hold down back home just as soon as I set you straight on a few things, as soon as you start showing what you're made of and fight back. This isn't the end of the world for you, it's just a little detour. Lots of people have detours of one kind or another and they live through them. You'll live through this.'

"Funny thing, but at that moment I was proud of my Mom and I didn't want to do anything to shame her. I began doing what I was supposed to do and started out on my new life. As it turned out, my upper extremities were not affected too much. I've never had garbled speech, never been blind, my sense of smell and taste have never gone. My hands have been paralyzed three different times but they've come back, though the feeling in them is not too good. The doctors were able to stop the fast rush of the paralysis and prevent my limbs from becoming deformed, but there has been a certain amount of permanent damage to the bowels, bladder, and lungs. Each year I am a bit more incapacitated than the year before, but live in the hope that science will soon find something to help me. In the meantime I live in a wheel chair and with a family that fortunately has a wonderful sense of humor and a fine philosophy of life. When I finally came home from the hospital they treated me like they always had, making light of the fact that I looked like a mechanical man with a corset for a back, hip-length braces, and crutches. We all took the attitude that I hadn't died because God had stopped it, He had things for me yet to learn and perhaps even things for me to do."

This is what happened to Jean Thoney in her own words—some of them brave words, all of them filled with a remarkable degree of self-knowledge. But all that happened some twenty years ago. Today, she is no longer a young girl in a wheel chair, but a middle-aged woman in a wheel chair. Twenty years of being an invalid could fray any family's nerves, break any girl's spirit. Has this happened?

Jean is home alone much of the time, long hours when she could mope and feel sorry for herself, if that were her nature. But listen to some excerpts from her letters to me:

"My parents had their vacation and I spent twelve days with my sister and it was a nice change, but believe me it was a change. My sister has a back porch off her upstairs bedroom and she put me out there for fresh air and so I could commune with nature, I guess. Nice thought and all well meant, but there was a big pear tree hanging over the porch and it was loaded with pears and birds. When the dear little creatures weren't knocking pears down on my head, they were dropping something else and after I was a complete mess I hollered uncle, and she came and took me inside. I'm a lover of nature but there's a limit and I've had it. . . .

"Someone is always telling me there's a new cure for multiple sclerosis. I used to try them all but now the word is Whoa! It isn't that I don't think they'll some day find a cure, because I do, but I'm just taking it easy on the curves, if you'll pardon the expression. This family is making damn sure before I try anything else that it isn't going to kill me, as a few in the past almost did. It's funny, I can't understand it, but I guess they want me around, multiple sclerosis and all. So you see, my family is just as crazy as I am . . .

"I am, my dear Lillian, sitting on top of the world, and I mean that literally. Callouses, you know. And what a place to have them! So the doctor taped airfoam pads over the callouses. I'm sitting on an airfoam pillow plus a rubber ring. Bouncy, to say the least. Anyway, I feel swell. My English teacher always told me 'swell' was only used for something swollen. Well, I still say I feel swell. I told you we never have a dull moment around here . . .

"In your last letter, Lillian, you put a postscript in which you said I was 'a strong, brave girl.' Strong? Well, not my bladder, I can tell you. Brave? Nuts. I just happen to enjoy life, even from a wheel chair, and if it's God's will that I be in one, the least I can do is to meet it the best way I know how. And after all, I have so much to be thankful for—a wonderful family and friends like you. I wonder if you have any idea of what your stepping into my life has meant to me? Your example, your courage, has given me so much. Maybe some day I'll be able to make you understand. Down deep in my heart I know I have no chance for recovery. Each year I lose a little ground. But then, don't we all? I just remember your advice to pray to God and keep smiling. I pray for you every day . . ."

There's a portrait of Jean Thoney in her own words, and they are beautiful and brave and very moving. She writes about three or four times a month and her letters are very precious to me. She says that I have helped her. It is the opposite. I feel shy before her strength, goodness, and beauty.

3

Darkness Will Pass

We are not always what we seem to be to others. The people who came to me with their troubles no doubt believed me to be a strong person. Yet, at the time I was, and I still am to a degree filled with the same emotional conflicts that most of us harbor in varying quantities. We all have our hopes, desires, dreams, and fears. Yet so much good was happening to me that my guilt was heavy when I did not try in some measure to lighten their burden. In a way this was difficult because I still had a rough road to travel and if I did not make it right to the very end, I would not be much good to myself or anyone else. Not everything is as it looks, either. In the eyes of my unseen friends, I had made it. Only I knew what a darn tough battle was in store for me.

Strangely, the people, the audiences, were much quicker

to accept me back than were the theatrical managers and booking agents. I remember I was living in Florida in 1953, when my life's story was done on the TV show "This Is Your Life," and from that moment on, the public opened their hearts and clamored to see me in person, yet jobs were very hard to get. It wasn't that the bookers were conspiring to prevent my comeback—they were just skeptical of my ability to continue to draw crowds. They considered me an overnight sensation who would fade just as fast.

Anyway, shortly after that TV show I began to do a tremendous business at the Clover Club in Miami for Jack Golden, the only man who had taken a chance with me. New York columnist Earl Wilson stopped by one night, saw my act, and said, "My goodness, Lillian, why aren't you in New York?"

"I'm just not getting any offers," I said.

"But look at the crowds you're drawing here!"

"I don't know the answer, Earl," I said. "Maybe they think a New York audience is different from a Miami audience."

When Earl returned to New York, he went directly to Monte Prosser at *La Vie en Rose* and told him I was breaking records in Florida. Monte was interested but it was six months before I got my big chance in New York. I was booked into *La Vie* in support of Julius La Rosa, who had just been "released" by Arthur Godfrey.

Julius is a fine artist, but this was his first New York

night-club engagement and I guess Monte was a little worried he might not carry it off alone with a sophisticated
audience. I was a sort of insurance, an old trouper who
could hold the show together if anything went wrong.
Well, nothing did. La Rosa was adorable, and the audience was wonderful to both of us. Also, something
quite surprising happened, something that was to be repeated again and again in the future, but this was the first
time. I was coming to the club one evening for the dinner
show and found a group of teen-agers with autograph
books clustered around the stage door. They were waiting
for La Rosa, I knew, so I hunched up my coat collar and
tried to sneak past them. I felt very diffident and unsure of
myself in front of those kids. I just didn't want them to
look at me and say to themselves, "Who is that old has-
been?" I was almost to the door when one of them spotted
me and squealed and they all descended upon me. They
were waiting for *me!* They wanted *my* autograph! Their
mothers before them had asked me for my signature, and
now they were doing the same thing. I could have kissed
every one of them. It was the first time in eighteen years
that I had given an autograph.

I was heartened by the way the people and the press accepted me and flocked to the shows. Monte threw his arms
about me and cried, "You've got to stay over, Lillian.
You've just got to. This is sensational!"

Burt and I thought that this was it! How little we knew!
After Julius played a week, I stayed on another week as

headliner and the bill held up beautifully. Then Monte suddenly said that he wanted someone else, someone who was then hot on records, to come in and he'd have me back in about four weeks.

I was drawing the crowds and I was convinced I would continue to draw them if he'd keep me on, but you can't run a man's business for him. And he was bringing me back for the entire month of March, 1954. Okay, another delay. But next time I'd really make it.

When March drew near, Monte decided he preferred an April booking, and then changed his mind to May. My book was scheduled to come out in June and I had made elaborate plans to hold a press party on its publication date and I wanted to be working at the time; I wanted to have my career back on an even keel. My agent, Buddy Howe, said, "What are you getting so excited about? You got a book coming, so what? A million books come out that nobody ever hears about. Don't count too much on it. Don't get yourself all riled up."

But I couldn't take his advice. It was more than just a job, it was my self-confidence that was involved. I had told all the press I would be back, and I didn't want to fail.

"I've got to work. I've got to!" I pounded my agent's desk.

"Sure, honey, sure," he said. Then he picked up the phone and called a man who owns one of the biggest clubs in the country. After he gave the pitch about me, he held the receiver so I could hear the answer.

"Who's interested in yesterday's history?" came the voice over the phone.

"Lillian wowed 'em up here in *La Vie*," Buddy said.

"Sure, but she's had it. She drew the crowd on a sympathy bit. I'm sorry, but for my money she's finished."

I did get some bookings, but they were all fill-ins. I played the *Chez Paree*, a smart spot in Chicago, but only because Helen Traubel decided not to stay on. At the end of this job Monte was still postponing my return to *La Vie* and so I went to the Elmwood Casino in Windsor, Canada. It was a large club, seating two thousand, and the management was afraid I might not fill it. Not many people there knew me because, I guess, "This Is Your Life" hadn't been seen in that area. But to everyone's amazement and mine, I did fill the room and the audiences were enthusiastic. The good Lord had given me a talent and I didn't deserve any credit for it, but on the other hand, if I failed to use and develop that gift, I deserved censure.

Well, I was certainly doing the best I could, and I knew the people liked me, but I still couldn't seem to get the break in New York where it was important. I kept thinking that if New York didn't want me, then I'd never successfully come back all the way.

Well, sometimes you just have to be tough. Sometimes you have to rear up and fight for your rights. I might have gone on for the rest of my life accepting fill-in bookings if I hadn't put my foot down at this moment. Or, to be more exact, if Burt hadn't. He went to our agent and Mr. Prosser and he said, "Lillian has a contract to return to *La Vie,* and by God, she's going to return!" And return I did. I went back with a salary increase from $750 to $1,500 a week. And business was excellent.

Right after *La Vie,* at the end of May, I went into the Palace Theater for the big Anniversary Show I mentioned earlier. It was not a two-a-day show with reserved seats and high prices, like Judy Garland's, who, after all, was still a big movie personality. But the people jammed the theater and kept coming back. They were not the New York sophisticates, but the middle-aged, middle-class couples from the Bronx and Brooklyn, and the teen-agers. On closing night, in a sudden and spontaneous demonstration, they began to throw flowers at me from the balconies. I literally had to dodge the bouquets as they fell to the stage, and I wept with thanksgiving as I did. The Palace management said they'd never seen anything quite like it.

That same week, I went on Ed Sullivan's TV show. My book was about to come out and I gave Ed a copy. He held it in his hand all through the show, even while he was introducing other acts. His generous gesture brought the book to the attention of millions of TV viewers.

That night Burt and I said once again that this time we had made it. But it wasn't quite the way we thought. There was a long road still ahead, with many a sharp turn and dangerous shoulder. The booking agents still took a dim view of my success. They thought it was a temporary phenomenon, that the crowds were coming to the clubs now out of curiosity and after once seeing me wouldn't return. Certainly the people I began to draw into the clubs were not always the usual nighttime habitués. Parents began to bring their children, saying in effect, "See her? We used to be her fans when we were your age." Priests and teachers and doctors came. More often than I can remember I was told that a psychiatrist was in the audience with a patient, both of them studying me. And there were always crowds of book readers who had finished *I'll Cry Tomorrow* and now wanted to see me smile in person.

The club owners were astounded by the crowds I was drawing, but it was not reflected in my financial standing. My salary remained at $1,500 a week, though I did business that often topped stars who received five times that amount. Now, fifteen hundred dollars may sound like a lot of money to many people, but the investment for my act had been tremendous. My musical arrangements cost anywhere from a thousand to fifteen hundred dollars a song. There were travel expenses, the pianist's salary, and clothes. One gown would at times cost me almost a week's salary—and I needed many. So my salary didn't leave me very much for any uncertain times that might come up.

There remained the problem of breaking through the prejudice some club owners have against an act that is modestly priced. I remember I tried to book into a club in New England and the owner said, "We want top talent here. At fifteen hundred you can't be very good." A couple of years later I did get a booking there for $7,000 a week and I asked him, "Do you think I'm better now?"

Despite everything, I was still looked on in the entertainment industry as a has-been, a lucky has-been with but a momentary place in the spotlight.

Please don't get the impression that I was unhappy or bitter during this period. I certainly wasn't. After all, I wasn't sure they were wrong about me. Maybe I would be just a flash in the pan. If so, it was a pretty big flash and I was grateful for it. I had lost sixteen years to alcohol and I was now receiving acclaim I never would have thought possible a short time before. And, in fact, I *was* making progress toward complete acceptance as an entertainer, even if at times it seemed at a snail's pace. Also there was the other side of my life that was growing richer day by day—the spiritual side. My book was a best seller and everywhere I went there were people who said it had been a source of inspiration to them. I was grateful for this, of course, but they were giving me much too much credit, measuring me far beyond my worth. It bothered me that people saw virtues in me I didn't believe I had. Actually, the most modest of us can help others if we really try. And I did try. Everywhere were people who needed another human being to take time to look at them and touch them and say to them that their lives were not without meaning, that their troubles would pass.

Such a girl was Clarice. I first received a letter from her

while I was playing the Mocambo in Los Angeles. She wrote:

"Dear Miss Lillian Roth, I really don't know how to start this letter except to tell you that I read *I'll Cry To-morrow* and I think you are a wonderful woman and I hope you can help my mother. She needs help so bad. You see, my mother has been drinking since she was fourteen and now she is thirty-six. She was not married when she had me and so I was taken away from her and don't live with her, but she's all I have in the world. I guess she hates me. She thinks I was the cause of all her trouble, but I wasn't even born at the time. I know I shouldn't tell you all this because you have your own troubles but I don't have anybody else to tell it to. I pray that some day I can have someone to love me so I can love them. It is all so lonely without anybody. My mother is drunk all the time and won't even talk to me when I try to help her. Please tell me what to do."

This letter was one of about fifty I received that day, and after reading it I had to lay it aside to go on with the rest of my mail. But it haunted me. One sentence marched back and forth in my mind: "I pray that some day I can have someone to love me so I can love them." The ache of that child's loneliness filled me. I picked up the letter again and found she lived just outside of Los Angeles. So I wrote her to come and visit me.

She came to my hotel room two days later. She was, I

guessed, about fifteen years old, and moved with the long-legged, awkward grace of a young colt. Her clothes were of sleazy material and the garish colors affected by a child who wishes desperately to be gay in appearance but has had no opportunity to develop taste. Her attire was forgotten, however, the moment I looked at her face. It was delicate, fine-textured, but pale with fright. The arch of her eyelids was so pronounced, it revealed the entire iris, giving her a naked and defenseless look.

I took a step toward her and at my smile her eyes filled with tears. I held out my arms and she ran to me and as I held her thin, convulsed body I thought that this was probably the first time in her life she had cried in another person's arms. Perhaps this in itself was help.

The first words she was able to speak were, "Everyone says 'like mother like daughter.' "

There it was, then, the core of her fears: If the mother had an illegitimate child, then the child in turn would turn bad; if the mother became an alcoholic, the child would inherit the problem.

Here was my old friend, the devil alcohol. This time, however, it was not only the alcoholic who was suffering, but the innocent child. If the mother had come, wanting help, I would have known what to say to her, but how could I comfort this lost child? I finally talked to her like an adult, hoping she would understand.

"You know I was once an alcoholic, don't you, Clarice?"

"Yes," she said, "I read it in your book."

"Why do you think I became one?"

She thought a moment. "Well, because you were un-happy."

"That was part of it, of course, but just part. There are all sorts of extenuating circumstances that contribute to alcoholism and some day we may have time to sit down and discuss them all. But you must remember that alcoholism is an illness, that your mother is ill, and this makes her lonely and unhappy. She doesn't hate you. She hates herself and what she is doing to you. No parent really hates his child or wants to hurt it. Can you understand that, Clarice?"

"I guess so." She thought a moment, her face still troubled, then said, "People keep saying I come from a bad line, that I have my mother's blood in me."

"Of course, you have your mother's blood, but that doesn't mean it's bad, and it certainly doesn't mean that you're going to turn out like your mother. Sometimes we inherit tendencies toward family weaknesses, but only tendencies and they don't have to develop into anything if we're careful and try to develop the best in us. The fact that your mother is having this difficulty is a good object lesson for you, something that will prevent you from turning into an alcoholic."

"Oh, it will," she said quickly, "it will."

"Just remember, my dear, that you are yourself and God never made anybody exactly like you. And nobody is ever going to force you to do anything you don't want to do.

You're going to make your own life, God gave you the freedom to do that, and it's going to be a fine one, I'm sure."

She looked at me wide-eyed, wanting to believe. I said, "We must try and help your mother, not because you're going to be like her, but because you're different, you're stronger than she is. And because you love her."

"You'll help her?"

"I'll try. You bring her to see me about this same time tomorrow afternoon."

"She might not come."

"I think she'll come if she knows you really love her, and you want her to come. Ask her and see."

They came, mother and daughter, the next afternoon. There were traces of beauty still left in the mother's face, and there was pride and hostility. We talked a long time and when she left I think she understood at least that I was not looking down upon her, censuring her, because I had once stood where she stood, perhaps a rung lower. In the end she agreed to meet with members of a local chapter of Alcoholics Anonymous. When they walked out, mother and daughter were holding hands.

I didn't see that child again until a year later, at a time when my own problems were so pressing that I had all but forgotten her. I didn't recognize her at first when she walked into my dressing room during a return engagement in Los Angeles, for she had gained both weight and poise. Gone was the haunted look, the over-dressing, the pathetic need to please.

She said, "I thought you'd like to know what happened to my mother."

"Indeed I would."

"We live together now, in a real nice apartment. She has a job and I have a job and, well, everything is just wonderful. She saw the A.A. people you sent us to and she hasn't had a drink in over ten months."

"And you're no longer afraid you'll turn out like her?"

She smiled. "Now I'd be proud to."

Many young people today are very concerned about drinking and morals in general. Some have seen a lot of drinking among their parents' generation and I think they want to avoid some of the mistakes. They're as full of life as we ever were, but I do think the world in constant crisis has made many of them quite serious about many things.

I remember particularly a visit I made to a parochial school in the South. I had left the Mocambo and was off on another tour of the night-club circuit when I received a letter from a nun who asked me if I could find time to come and address her high-school class on the problems of drink. She sent the cutest note, trying to be modern and frank without offending, explaining that she imagined her students didn't believe she knew much about the evils of whiskey and she thought an authority on the subject would have more influence with them. At the end of her letter, she wrote, "If it wouldn't be too much trouble, could you sing a song or two for us. I want my boys and girls to learn something from you, but I'd like them to have a good time, too."

I have met a lot of nuns, and they are kind and good and among the most dedicated people in the world. I've seen poverty nuns, "Little Sisters of the Poor," scrubbing the floors of a janitor's quarters while he was away at work. And the medical nuns—what comfort and skill they bring to the sick. These women are truly the servants of God and the people, and their childlike simplicity and goodness touches your heart. Naturally, I accepted the invitation.

The student president and the treasurer of the high-school class called at my hotel to escort me to the school. In the auditorium, I met the nun who had written to me, a gentle, smiling woman. Several other nuns and priests stood around the edge of the room while I talked to the students. I didn't give any "do's" or "don't's" but just tried to explain what had happened to me. I told these youngsters that I was like them once, in school, and aware that there was such a thing as drunkenness, but never had the slightest idea it could happen to me. A lot of people seemed to think I became an alcoholic because as a child star I was in show business. That just wasn't true, because my mother took care of me as well as any mother ever did, maybe she was even a little stricter and more protective than most. My sister, too, was in show business with me, she had the same background, and she didn't become an alcoholic. No, it depends on the individual, I explained to them, and then I gave a few signposts they should watch out for. I didn't go into it too heavily, I wanted to be educational but not depressing. I just wanted to plant a few seeds that could one day blossom if necessary.

My accompanist, Dick Wess, had come along and now sat at a battered upright piano. I gave him a signal and we did a few songs. I thought to myself that I had to be careful and not work too broadly, but I was certain they'd enjoy the bounce and gaiety of some of the modern songs. They did, indeed. The nuns applauded as enthusiastically as the students.

My accompanist then played a couple of solo pieces, some Brahms and a Chopin Etude. When he had finished, there was applause. Then a young nun in the back of the room spoke up and asked if Dick could play some boogie woogie. Everybody cheered and Dick gave them some fine barrel-house piano.

We had tea and cakes and a lot of the students gathered around for an informal question-and-answer period. I didn't always have all the answers, but I did the best I could. One boy wanted to know if I thought cigarettes were bad. I had to tell him that I personally didn't think smoking cigarettes was bad morally, though I knew that some religions did hold that view. It was more a question of health, in my opinion, and if he could wait a few years before smoking, he'd be a lot healthier.

A girl said, "Miss Roth, the boy I'm going with seems to think I'm a poor sport if I don't take a drink. I don't want him to think that."

I said, "Maybe that boy isn't very serious about you. When a boy is really serious, when he is in love with a girl and thinking of one day marrying her, he doesn't want her to drink and make a spectacle of herself. And the truth is, you can have a brighter, gayer time at a party when you're not drinking, when you're just yourself. I think that's what a fine boy wants, a girl he can look at with pride and say, 'There's nothing artificial about her. She's herself and that's for me.' "

A boy said, "I'm going to take a drink next week, on New Year's Eve. Don't you think that's all right?"

"How old are you?"

"Sixteen," he said. "But just on New Year's Eve. That can't be wrong, can it?"

"Can you hardly wait?" I asked.

He grinned. "Yeah, I can hardly wait."

"Then I wouldn't take it. When it's a *must*, then it's a *shouldn't*. That's one of the danger signals to watch for, the anticipation, the need for a drink. When a drink doesn't mean too much to you, when you can take it or leave it, then you have no problem."

A dark-eyed Italian boy of seventeen said to me, "We

drink wine with our meals and always have. Do you think that is wrong?"

He had me there. There are people who for generations have consumed a lot of alcoholic beverages without apparent ill effects—the Germans and their beer, the Italians and their wine. I don't know for certain, but I would guess that the rate of alcoholism in Germany or Italy is no higher than here in America. So what could I say to this boy?

"Do you eat your food or do you favor the wine?" I asked.

"Oh, I eat a lot. I've got a good appetite. But we drink wine like some people drink coffee."

I grinned at him. "As long as your food desire is the greater I don't think you have too much to worry about."

The questions came thick and fast. But I went away feeling all warm and good inside.

I often think of those nuns trying to cope with the world's sordidness, trying to lead youth without themselves ever having experienced the pitfalls they warn against. Actually, they are wise women and know a great deal about life, but they also know that the testimony of one who has actually fallen is often more effective than anything they can say. But I do believe that the very goodness of these women inspires the boys and girls who come into contact with them.

Whatever the reasons for it, I think the problem of alcoholism is probably much less prevalent among young people today than it was among my generation, twenty-five years ago. I am not a doctor or a sociologist or an expert on anything except Lillian Roth (and sometimes not much of an expert on her), but my experience and my mail indicates that today's youth is generally pretty clear-headed about drinking and morals in general.

No, the parents and not the children face the terrible crisis. One morning, a letter arrived in the mail from an Indiana wife and mother. It is typical of so many letters I receive that I want to quote from it:

"Dear Miss Roth: I am sending this letter hoping that you will read it personally, not some secretary. I know that is asking a lot of someone who is so busy as you are but I'm desperate and don't know anyone to turn to except you. I am a Christian woman (Protestant) married to a habitual drunk for thirteen years and have five children. Now we have nothing, not even the essentials that it takes to live, although I would be satisfied with even that if my husband only wanted to help himself. My minister has talked to him, the entire congregation of my church has prayed for him, but it doesn't seem to help . . . I don't really know why I'm writing this letter except that maybe God will help me to make you understand that I do need help for my husband . . .

"I have begged him to contact a doctor or the A.A. group before it is too late, but he refuses to do anything. He gets drunk for days at a time and just lies around the house and fights with his family if we say anything or go near him. They say he has to want help from A.A. before they will come to him and he doesn't want it, so what can I do? . . .

"He makes plenty where he works, *when* he works, and we could have the essentials in life if he'd only stay off the liquor. Now we are so terribly behind in our bills and this Monday they are going to turn off our gas and electricity and we heat with gas and so I don't know what I'll do about my children in the cold house. We owe four or five months and they just won't carry us any longer, and I can't say I blame them. I can't even buy my children the clothes they need to go outdoors and we have to divide up what we have so that only a couple at a time can be seen in public . . .

"And instead of my husband facing the situation and trying to help himself, he begins to feel sorry for himself and gets drunk all the more so he won't see what's going on. I'm not writing all this for your sympathy but so you will see the situation and maybe give me some solution. There must be something to do that I haven't yet tried. Just tell me. I'll try anything. Sincerely, Mrs.——."

How many thousands of homes are darkened just as this one? How many thousands of wives and mothers have wept and prayed and despaired? And how many husbands have looked at their defeats and guilts and found them insupportable, except with a glass of whiskey in hand? In my mail alone there are thousands of such cases. Again let me say that I am no authority on this problem of alcoholism, I do not speak as a representative of A.A., but within my knowledge and experience I want to list the most common questions and my answers about A.A.:

Q.: What does A.A. mean?

A.: Alcoholics Anonymous. A group of people sharing the common problem of alcoholism who have gotten together to help each other.

Q.: What does it do?

A.: Through group therapy it arrests the illness and in seventy percent of the cases brings about recovery.

Q.: Why anonymously?

A.: Until the public is fully educated to the problem, alcoholics prefer to keep their identity unknown. Through my own observations and information, gained by traveling and meeting people all through the United States and Australia, there is a far greater awareness and understanding today than when I joined A.A. in 1946.

Q.: Is A.A. a club?

A.: No. It is an informal society with no officers, no dues, and no laws. It is not an organization, it is a fellowship. The only requirement necessary to join is a sincere desire to stop drinking.

Q.: Who is eligible?

A.: Alcoholics only.

Q.: Is it a cure?

A.: No. To date nothing has been discovered medically

that has proved to be a positive cure, but the alcoholic can stop drinking for all time on a day-to-day basis.

Q.: Is A.A. church-sponsored?

A.: No. There are no ties or affiliations with any one church, though many members of the clergy recommend A.A. Alcoholics who have fallen away eventually return to their folds through the spiritual movement in A.A.

Q.: Aren't alcoholics usually down-and-outers?

A.: Certainly not. Alcoholism is considered a disease and, therefore, it is no respecter of people. They come from all walks of life and are a cross-section of the population.

Q.: I have a relative who needs A.A. Will they save him?

A.: A.A. is not a rescue squad. The call for aid must come from the alcoholic. A.A. cannot be forced upon an alcoholic.

Q.: Aren't alcoholics just plain drunks?

A.: No. All drinkers do not become alcoholics, but all alcoholics get drunk.

Q.: How many alcoholics would you estimate in the United States?

A.: It is claimed that there are about four and one-half million. About five percent of the people who drink, whether it be social, light, or heavy, become alcoholics.

Q.: Are requests or letters that are sent to A.A. kept confidential?

A.: Absolutely and entirely.

Q.: When was A.A. founded?

A.: About 1935. Statistics show that since that date about sixty to seventy percent of A.A.'ers have had successful sobriety.

Q.: Do all alcoholics stay sober once they join A.A.?

A.: At the outset about fifty percent make it without slipping—A.A.'s expression for returning to drink. Of the fifty percent who have trouble, about twenty-five percent return to A.A.

Q.: Why don't all alcoholics recognize their stupidity and do something about it?

A.: Because they are sick people. They have a physical allergy coupled with a mental obsession. They may be rational on any subject but alcoholism. Their will has been broken. They have as little control over their illness as the hay-fever victim does over goldenrod.

Q.: Does A.A. believe in prohibition?

A.: As a group, A.A. has no opinion on the subject. They are not reformers; they merely try to help the alcoholic get a new lease on life without alcohol.

Q.: Are all meetings closed to non-alcoholics?

A.: No. A.A. has open meetings for families, friends, and anyone interested in the problem, including students, lawyers, and doctors.

Q.: How does one know he is an alcoholic?

A.: Go to a few meetings and listen to the speakers. It

is better to be at A.A. and wonder if you are an alcoholic than to be in jail or an institution and know you are one.

If the above questions and answers are for the relatives and friends of the alcoholic, these words are for him alone: I know you are the most depressed and miserable person in the world, for you are in the process of losing life's most precious possessions: family, friends, position, self-respect, and perhaps in the end even your sanity. I know your anxiety about tomorrow, your remorse for yesterday. I know the terror that comes after an alcoholic binge—it is beyond description. I know the sick, trembling, retching body, the strangulation of the throat, the thunderous heart palpitations, the horror of seen and unseen things, the shattered nerves screaming in agony, "Oh God, what horrible thing did I do yesterday, the day before, the years before? God help me, help me."

But with all the terror and all the remorse, it is not easy to stop drinking. I know that too. Perhaps, however, I can make a few suggestions that may help:

Don't feel sorry for yourself, or envious of those who can drink. Just remember that you are not alone in your problem. When you say to yourself, "Joe can have a drink without trouble, why not I?" just think of all the "I's" who can't.

Be grateful that your illness is something you can arrest by simply not picking up that first drink of the day. There are many people sick with other diseases who would gladly change places with you and your simple prescription.

Remember that in your case a drink is a drunk. You were a long time drinking and the obsession for alcohol does not leave overnight. Start out by counting the blessings that sobriety will bring you: freedom from shame, contempt, pity, and aid; the ability to live once again in the light instead of behind drawn shades; a soaring spirit that can face the truth about yourself; peace of mind, serenity, the regaining of your lost dignity, love for God and man.

If you keep these advantages in mind, hope will begin to live in your heart. Hope is the most important of all, and those of us who have regained our sobriety can promise you that it is possible to fulfill that hope. Remember: 1) Be honest with yourself and others; 2) Control the emotions that lead to drink; 3) Eliminate self-pity that causes melancholia; 4) Help someone—it helps you.

Soon your desire for alcohol will leave and the only consciousness you will have of liquor will be the compassion you feel when you witness a suffering person who drinks the way you used to.

4

The Void Inside

I have learned that what binds us together in love is not so much shared happiness as shared sorrow. I first began to understand this fully one night, shortly after my book was published, when a young man, who had organized a Lillian Roth fan club in his home town, came one-hundred-and-ninety miles to see me where I was playing a hotel date. I had no idea he was coming until his name was sent up from the lobby, just before the dinner show. I told him I was dressing and that if he'd wait in the lobby for me I'd soon be down and take him into the show as my guest.

When I went to the lobby, I found a dark-haired, slender young man of eighteen or nineteen, with a sensitive face and a diffident smile. There was a camera slung around his neck, and I posed for a couple of pictures.

Following the show I met him again and took him to a sofa in the corner of the lobby for a chat. He told me about the Lillian Roth fan club in his town and how all their dues were given over to a local charity. It was clear to me that he was not just a stage-struck youngster but a very nice and serious young man. Suddenly, however, his words faltered and I looked at him to discover that his eyes were full of tears.

When I asked him what was wrong, he couldn't seem to answer, partly, I knew, because he was in an agony of embarrassment. People in the lobby were beginning to look at us and so I took him by the arm and led him to the deserted dining room. When we were alone, he stammered out an apology.

"I'm sorry . . ."

"There's nothing to be sorry for. My husband is a grown man and I've seen him cry, so it's nothing to be ashamed of. But tell me what is wrong."

He shook his head and turned away to try and stem the tears.

"Perhaps I can help if you'll tell me," I said.

"I . . . I don't know what's wrong. It's just that I suddenly felt so terribly sad about . . . I don't know . . . just about everything."

"It may seem about everything, but it's probably not."

"Well," he grinned at me ruefully, "it may not make any sense, but part of it was gladness, too."

"It makes sense," I nodded.

He said, "I was glad that *you* were not lonely. Maybe I was feeling sorry for myself, but I wasn't jealous or envious of you . . . I was really glad that you had friends and success . . . and everything."

I was beginning to understand. I probed gently, "And you don't have any of these things?"

He shrugged his shoulders. "I suppose I have as much as any guy my age. I've got a father and mother and sister who are all okay. And I do all right in school. I've organized this Lillian Roth fan club that does good work. But . . ." he shook his head in bewilderment, "I still feel so all alone. I can't explain it."

"You mean that nobody really and truly seems to understand what you are deep inside . . . and that's where you're lonely?"

"Yes . . . yes, that's about it."

"And you're happy for me because I don't have that loneliness, that void. But you're so terribly wrong. I'm not different from you."

He seemed startled, unbelieving. He had seen me surrounded by people, apparently admired and loved, and so he ached in that sad-gladness I know so well, but he was wrong. We talked for a long time that evening and I tried to make him see that all people go through life with that void inside them. One day he would probably fall in love and get married, but even that would probably not banish entirely

[71]

the feeling of aloneness, of lostness. But in marriage there could be a companionship of that very aloneness, sadness, one for the other. I hoped he understood what I was trying to say.

I believe that the great common denominator that ties one man to another is sorrow. It is not the happy-happy talk that lets us reach another human heart, but a shared hurt or fear or defeat. It is compassion that draws us together. Within us there seems to be an aching, a frightening void we are forever trying to fill, but never quite do. I suppose the Freudians would say it is a desire to return to the womb; the formal religionists would explain that it is need to return to our Maker; in either case the void seems to remain during life. I'm not smart enough to know who is right, but I do know that the void is within everyone of us, and that we seek each other out in an effort to fill it. We need love and tenderness; we need even someone's sad heart. I have only to look at my own marriage to know this is true. I'm not referring to my first four marriages (a record I'm not proud of), but my last, real one to Burt McGuire.

Burt and I were both alcoholics. We met in the A.A. movement, we helped each other find sobriety and maintain it over the past twelve years. We have shared a rather tumultuous existence with pretty, glittering successes, but as I look back on our life together, the things I remember with a throat-tightening tenderness are the defeats and the sorrows we shared. It is from them that love is distilled and the void filled—at least partially. I'd like to tell you about some of them.

It was Burt who insisted that I could have a comeback in my theatrical career, and in 1946, before we were married, helped me get one of my first night-club bookings. It was in a club in a Canadian town, and I made the trip up there alone with great apprehension. I had only been in A.A. for about three months, and I felt very jittery and unsure of myself. The club turned out to be a bleak one, on a back street, but at least I was the star of the show and it gave me a thrill to see my name upon the boards again. The house orchestra consisted of a saxophone, a piano, and drums, and during rehearsal I received the most ragged sort of accompaniment. But then I guess my stage presence was pretty ragged too. I was in no position to demand special attention from the musicians, or even any enthusiasm in their tootling and pounding. We went through a couple of standards once or twice, and then I stepped down from the stage and started to leave the club.

"Just a minute, girlie," the club owner called. "We ain't through with you yet."

"I think the musicians know my songs all right," I said.

"Stick around. We use you with the comedian for a black-out skit at the end of the show."

My contract didn't provide for my services in any skit, but who was I to stick to the letter of the contract? I was lucky to have a job without standing on my rights. I took a seat in the empty club and waited through the rest of the rehearsal of the dancing numbers and the comedian's routine. When it ended, I heard the club owner call out from the back of the room, "Okay, Roth, on stage."

"What am I supposed to do in this black-out?"

"I'll explain the scene," he said. "This is the bedroom of Reggie Van Got-rocks, millionaire playboy. While he's been away from home his wife has hired a new maid . . . that's you, Roth. When Reggie comes home drunk he mistakes you for a hall tree and hangs his hat on your left . . ."

He demonstrated the action by jumping up on the stage and draping a hat on my bosom. I snatched it off. "I . . . I'm sorry," I said, "but I can't do that."

"Don't worry, kid, you got the equipment for it. Besides, we'll sew a hook on your dress to make sure the hat is caught."

"No, I'm sorry, but I can't do it. I can't be in the skit."

"What're you talkin' about? Why can't you do it? Why can't you be in the black-out?"

"Because it's in bad taste and I . . . I just can't do it."

"Bad taste?" His eyes widened in disbelief. Then his voice dripped with sarcasm. "I guess I made a mistake, huh? I guess we got a lady here, someone who's been brought up by governesses in a castle, someone who don't know the meaning of a four-letter word, someone who's never been in the gutter. My mistake. All the time I thought I'd hired Lillian Roth."

I stood tense and trembling, close to tears, hearing the

derisive snickers from the orchestra. He kept at me, making fun of me, trying to bully me into doing the skit, and I kept saying no.

Finally he threw up his arms in exasperation and said, "Please, your ladyship, just do me one favor. Why all of a sudden are you so high and mighty? Why is everything here suddenly in bad taste? Why can't you do it?"

What could I say to him? I wasn't putting on false airs, I was just being myself. I had never in my life used "blue" material, and I couldn't bring myself to do it now, no matter how badly I needed the job. But I knew he'd laugh at me if I said that. He'd point out the fact that I had been a drunk, been in the gutter, so who was I to draw the line? I wouldn't be able to make him understand that my alcoholism had been a sickness, not an immorality or a vulgarity, that with all that had happened to me, I had never become hard inside.

Also, now that I had stopped drinking and was trying to come back, it was doubly important to me that I regain my dignity.

I stood there stubbornly and said, "I can't do it. I just can't."

He stormed and raved but finally ended the rehearsal without the skit. Shaken, I went to my hotel for a few hours of rest before the opening show. When I returned to the club that night, I found all the signs had been repainted, dropping my name from starring position to the bottom of the list, and in the smallest lettering of all. And during the first show the musicians were not only ragged in their accompaniment, but indifferent to the beat. I sang with as much heart as I could, but finally I fled from the stage in tears.

I grabbed my coat from my dressing room and ran outdoors to gulp down the cold, clean night air. But it didn't help. I ran all the way to my hotel room, slammed the door, and leaned against it. Now my fear was not of failure at the club, but of something else. This was a situation where people of my psychological and chemical make-up turn to the bottle. Could I get by without it?

With a sinking heart I watched myself as one by one the old symptoms came back to me. First I broke out in a cold sweat. I began to tremble, and I had trouble swallowing and breathing. My jaw was stiff, as if gripped in some sort of paralysis. Zooming and whirling spots swarmed about my head, as if I were being attacked by an armada of tiny, colored airplanes. Nausea churned in my stomach.

It seemed that only a drink of whiskey would force open my closing throat and relieve the gagging, the suffocating; that only whiskey could warm my stomach, stop the trembling and the cold sweat. But even as my body cried out for the drink, my mind stood apart and was aghast, knowing what the result would be. But the thirst grew and grew; the sound part of my mind was being overwhelmed by the neurotic part of it, and by the chemical need of my body. It was too much to fight alone. I tottered to the bed, fell upon it, and reached a palsied hand for the phone. I telephoned Burt in New York.

The moment he heard my voice he knew what the trouble was. Without hesitation he said, "I'll come right up, Lillian. Just hang on. I'll be there within six hours."

"Six hours!" I wailed. "Oh God . . ."

"If you can't make the six hours, hang on for six minutes, and then another six minutes."

"I'll try . . ."

I lived through hell during those next six hours. There were moments so bad I stripped the bed and ripped the sheets into tiny ribbons, tearing the cloth to match the tearing that was going on inside me. At last the door opened and there was Burt. At the sight of him, I collapsed into hysterical tears which continued for a good half-hour, while he sat beside me on the bed and held my hand and talked to me.

Finally, when I was able to control myself, he reached for the hotel Bible and we began to read together. We read from Isaiah: "They that wait upon the Lord shall renew their strength; they shall mount up with wings as eagles; they shall run, and not be weary; and they shall walk, and not faint."

When Burt closed the Bible he said, "All right, let's go talk to that guy."

"Burt, how can I walk over to that club? I'm ashamed to face them."

"You have nothing to be ashamed of."

"I'm ashamed of myself. I'm sick inside, and I'm scared, and that makes me ashamed."

Burt stood up. "I'll go talk to him alone. I'll tell him he can't do this to you."

He started toward the door, limping on his bad leg that had been damaged by polio, and as I watched him I felt a tightening around my heart. Burt was not a well man, any more than I was a well woman. He too had been on the wagon for only a brief eight months, and prior to that he had suffered the same tortures I had known. His wealthy and socially prominent family had disowned him. When I met him in Alcoholics Anonymous, he had been sleeping on the waiting room benches of Pennsylvania Station. Having been born a blue-blood with his name in the Social Register, perhaps his humiliation and bewilderment had been even greater than mine. Certainly at this stage his security in his new-found sobriety could be no firmer than mine, yet he had the courage to take on my troubles. I could hardly let him do the whole job. I stood up and followed him out of the room.

The night-club owner was a sadistic bully. He towered over Burt, blowing cigar smoke in his face and sneering at him. He called me all the foul names, thinking that Burt could do nothing because of his affliction. As I listened I felt terrible that Burt had to endure this abuse because of me. At the end Burt said quietly, "Some day Miss Roth will be a great star and you'll regret this."

"Right now," the club owner retorted, "she's a drunk and a has-been, and she's working for me."

We walked slowly back to the hotel, feeling terribly depressed and almost physically battered. "What am I going to do, Burt?"

"Finish out the engagement," he said.

"With everybody laughing at me? With my act and billing cut to shreds?"

"Yes, even under those conditions. You must try to do it, Lillian. I'll stay in town, if it will help."

"If it will help!" I gave a mirthless laugh. Without Burt at my side it would be inconceivable. I had held out six hours without him, but if it had been six hours and ten minutes I think I would have gone mad, or have taken a drink which would have led to the same thing.

Burt's confidence in me sustained me. I stayed on and completed my engagement right to the last show and never once did the black-out skit. Burt's faith in me gave me courage, but it was the humiliation he received at the club owner's hands that touched my heart. We had been bruised together, and we reached for each other to heal the hurt.

We left Canada and came back to New York for an engagement at a club, since closed, called the *Chateau*, on Fifty-second Street. I felt certain this was an important break on my comeback road. It was a small club, but it was located between Fifth and Park Avenues, and I had been told it had a select clientele. Here was the type of place where I could be re-"discovered" by some important producer, I thought. I was terribly excited and hopeful.

When I arrived there, I found it wasn't smart at all, and few producers would be found dead in it. Some people did see me, however, including an agent I had known years ago. I'll call him Jim.

He came backstage and said, "I may be able to get you a few weeks here and there around town if you sign with me."

"No thanks, Jim," I said, "I don't think I should sign. I've had a few offers and I don't want to do anything to lose them. I've got a guest shot coming up at *La Martinique* and . . ."

"Don't be a fool," he snorted. "That won't lead to anything. I've got influence in this town and I can place you, but if you don't sign with me, you won't get a job in a hash house. Now get smart, Lillian."

"Not now, Jim. Maybe later. I'm going to work on my comeback slowly and . . ."

"Comeback? Ha! You're too old for a comeback. There's a dozen young singers around town twice as good as you are and fifteen years younger. Who needs you? You'll only get work if you sign with me and I use my influence in the right places."

I wanted to cry, but all I said was, "No, Jim."

He looked at me for a moment with a sneer on his face, then said, "Lillian, you're a has-been."

I went on and did my Sunday night guest shot at *La Martinique* and the audience was so enthusiastic that the club owner decided to engage me for the following week.

That first week was very good and I received some fine reviews, especially from Earl Wilson, Lee Mortimer, and *Variety*, and the owner decided to hold me over for a second week. This time I shared billing with Katheryn Dunham and her dancers.

I admired Miss Dunham and we became friends. She had nothing to do with the unhappy events that followed. My first suspicion that something might be wrong came when I saw the agent, Jim, huddling with the club owners. I knew he was Dunham's agent and had booked her into *La Martinique*. He was now talking about me, I felt sure. Soon I was certain.

The owner called me into his office, a cubbyhole lined with photographs of performers and all of them autographed to him with fond words.

"Lillian," he said, "you don't fit very well on an all-Negro bill."

"I don't know why not."

"*You* don't know why not? *You* don't have to know, I'm tellin' you."

"I've got a contract for this week," I said firmly, but my heart was pounding. If I could just hold out another week in New York I might get my comeback rolling. I needed the money, too. I was afraid that a cancellation would make the bookers think I was drinking again and unable to go on. "It's valid. The union will back me up."

"Okay, okay, don't get so high and mighty. You're still nothing but a lush."

I choked back any retort.

He said, "As of tonight, you're cut to two songs. You open the show."

That evening I told Burt, "Now I'm a dog act."

Burt pretended to laugh. "Don't you worry. You're going to be terrific."

He was always full of confidence, full of encouragement. It made me feel sad and guilty because I was letting him down. But maybe he was right. Maybe . . .

After that night's show the owner came to me and said, "You're no good in the opening, Lillian. Like I told you, you don't fit into this show."

"I've got a contract," I said.

"Yeah, and you're a lawyer. At the midnight show you go on at intermission. See if you like that!"

After the midnight show he came into my dressing room and leaned against the wall to look at me with great disgust. Finally he said, "I don't know what to do with you. You're really lousy."

I had braced myself for his words, but still they came like a blow in the stomach. I felt my throat constrict and my jaw muscles tighten. Through my mind raced the thought that a drink was what I needed. A drink would relax my throat and let me breathe. I had been dry for only a short time and my body still cried for alcohol at each emotional crisis. I needed a drink. Maybe I was lousy, the way he said. Maybe it was all useless to try and return to show business. Oh, how I needed a drink.

I heard him leave and I ran to the dressing table and clung to it, shutting my eyes, praying for the spell to pass. But it got worse. I broke into a sweat and began to tremble. A drink—oh God, no! I looked in the mirror and saw a wild, gaunt face. I closed my eyes, feeling sick.

Then it came to me—the snatch of a song. I reached for it, began to hum it brokenly.

"When you walk through the storm, keep your chin up high . . . Walk on, walk on, with hope in your heart and you'll never walk alone."

With a sob I sat down. The spell had passed.

A few moments later, Burt walked into the room. He saw how white and drained I looked and sat on the edge of the table to hold my hand, hard. I felt so ashamed that I had failed him.

"You had a spell," he said.

I nodded, miserable.

"But it passed. You were alone and you conquered it."

"I knew you were coming. I wasn't alone because you were near."

He said firmly, "You made it alone this time. Remember that. And be proud of it."

For the rest of the week they kept pushing me around at the club, first in one spot on the bill and then in another, trying to undermine my confidence so I'd quit. I got very nervous and my vocal chords kept tightening, making me hoarse. When they heard my hoarseness, they turned on the cooling system right over my head during my act to make it worse.

In the middle of the week, Jim came in one evening with another act of his to try out. They decided to put it on in my place, knowing that it would break my spirit.

"Your voice is no good, Lillian," the owner said. "You're not going on tonight."

When it came time for the show he suddenly turned to me and said, "Why aren't you dressed?"

"You said I wasn't going on tonight," I replied.

"I said no such thing. You're just trying to louse up the show. I'm calling the union right now and make a formal complaint that you're not ready to perform and the contract is voided."

When the union representative arrived I said to him, "Maybe I'm not up on a couple of union rules, but I certainly haven't been trying to ruin this show and I've been ready to go on every night."

After listening to both sides, the union representative said to the club owner, "She's a little hoarse from nervous strain but she's able to do a show. Her contract stands."

What this meant was that the club would have to pay me for the rest of the week, but it didn't mean they had to let me perform. And they didn't. Every night I'd get dressed and made-up, then just about at the time for my cue they'd announce I wasn't going on.

They dropped my name from the ads, from the posters in front, from the marquee. Anybody who called me—newspapermen and old acquaintances—would receive the answer that they didn't know where I was, and of course, in many people's minds this meant I was back on the bottle.

Katheryn Dunham called me into her dressing room and said, "Lillian dear, I feel so very bad about what they're doing to you. I wish there was some way I could help you." She took my hand in hers.

The week ended and so did my engagement, my non-appearing engagement. With it ended my chance for a comeback in New York for many a long, heartbreaking year. Burt was with me that last day, God bless him, and he took up his job of fortifying me.

"Lillian, we both knew the road back was going to be a rocky one. To have come into New York the very first time and hit it big, well, maybe that would have been too easy a victory. Maybe you have to prepare longer, work harder. But one thing I know for certain, you're going to make it."

As he talked on I thought that maybe this boy really loved me. He was trying to help me, I was sure, and he must love me, too. My heart warmed with the knowledge.

Burt had fought his way back, he was sober and now he

had enough strength for both of us. I would be ashamed not to carry some of my own burden. I'd try. I'd try for his sake as well as my own. The following month, January 1947, we were married.

I don't want to give the impression that this was a marriage consummated only out of sorrow and sympathy, for that was not the case at all. It was a shared hurt that made us tender with each other, that allowed each of us to approach the core of the other without fear. But in marriage we also pooled our strengths, our hopes, and our laughter. Burt's perseverance was always greater than mine. Thank God for that.

He is a man with a very obvious infirmity, for he limps badly on his polio-wracked leg, and his right arm is also affected, yet he walks with dignity. He refuses to give in to his disability, refuses to walk cautiously searching the terrain in front of him, and because he holds his head up, he sometimes stumbles over obstructions and takes nasty falls. But he always pulls himself erect and continues walking as if nothing had happened. His right foot is extremely tender and requires special orthopedic shoes, and whenever anybody steps on it the agony is excruciating. Yet I have never heard Burt utter a word of complaint.

One of his strengths is his logical mind. I am emotional, and it is good that he is not shaken by my storms, that he can stand aside and guide me with a cool, sure perception of the proper road. On the other hand, my emotionalism is good for him, it supplies an outlet that he, with his rigid self-control, cannot allow himself. We balance and complement each other. We have both known tragedy, and this has tempered us, given us, I hope, a certain wisdom about life, an understanding of each other.

Burt had been a very talented and successful man in advertising and sales promotion before his alcoholism, and now that we were both sober it did seem natural for him to return to his work. However, he understood how important it was for my mental health that I make a comeback in my profession and he gave up all thoughts of his own career to help me re-establish myself. He worked out a plan: the first step in fighting our way back to the top was to achieve success in the night-club circuit. Burt's strength and determination were such that I came to believe it possible, and we began to live our lives in daily preparation for the new successes. It would be nice to say that together we swept up the comeback trail, clear-eyed, sure-footed, and triumphant. But that was not the way it happened.

We stumbled, we faltered, and I was afraid.

For three years we fought for bookings in the better clubs, and though I worked quite a bit, it all led nowhere. The people who came to see and hear me were good to me, but news of their warmth didn't filter up to the big booking agents and I didn't get steady work. And pretty soon even the small bookings petered out.

In 1947, as I already told in *I'll Cry Tomorrow*, Burt and I went to Australia. I say "went" when it really should be "fled," for at the time everything seemed just too much for me. I still had not been able to find quietude of mind. Inside, I was sick to death. I hated what I had been and, contrary to public opinion, every time I answered an interview about my alcoholism, I died a little. Yet, I suppose that the deep imprints of the past are the stepping stones into the future.

I can't say that the eight months in Australia did much for my comeback, professionally, but I became the channel through which many groups of Alcoholics Anonymous were formed. Once the word went out through a magazine story that I was a member of A.A., my name became a household word throughout the country. Nevertheless, it is hard to make people differentiate between the famous and the infamous. I did not want people to come to my performances because I had done some work for A.A. There is no glory in being a glorified alcoholic. I was grateful for the friendship and love given to us by so many good people, and I shall always remember Australia with a fondness in my heart. But my career was still in dead center when we left for home. Maybe this time, we hoped, Hollywood would notice us.

The day before we sailed, Burt looked at me with a speculative eye and said, "You know, Lillian, the girls in Australia are big-framed and next to them you look petite. Well, you look shorter, anyway, but not much narrower. But back in Hollywood they're going to be smaller and narrower both."

"A long way of saying I'm heavy, huh?"

He grinned. "Pleasingly plump for my eyes, but for the eyes of those booking agents . . ."

"I know, I know."

"What do you say we take off a few pounds during the boat trip back?"

"*We!*" I snorted. "You with all of your hundred-and-twenty-two pounds. It's easy for you to talk. But you're right, of course."

This was the first time Burt had mentioned my weight because all during those months in Australia it had been necessary for me to eat a lot to build up shattered nerve tissues. But now, he figured, I was well enough to get myself back into an acceptable silhouette. I knew he was right, much as I was going to miss the pies and cakes and ice cream which had become alcohol's understudy—concentrated sugar.

It was a long and tortuous trip across the Pacific on a slow boat. The heat was fierce, and I became sick with hives, but I was determined to allow nothing to interfere with my reducing program. Every day I appeared on deck for exercises. The sun was blistering and the steel deck-plates became so hot they seared my feet right through my shoes. No one else was foolish or desperate enough to appear on deck during the day. There were some acrobats and weight-lifters aboard and I used their equipment, struggling for hours with bars and dumbbells. Sometimes the heat reached a hundred-and-thirty degrees.

Nights were even worse, for I was separated from Burt for the first time since our marriage. We had to live in male and female dormitories, and I occupied a cabin with twenty other women. The bunks were tiered three high and mine was the bottom one. There was a single small fan in the cabin which hardly stirred the heavy, fetid air. I'd crawl into my oven-like bunk, sweating and itching, and begin a night-long battle against the smothering feeling of claustrophobia.

Another horror was added. During the first night, at about eleven thirty, I heard a quick, sharp cry and then muffled whimpering. It continued for ten minutes, perhaps, then subsided only to begin again. This went off and on throughout the night, always the sharp little cry followed by whimpering. I hung onto my bunk and prayed that I wasn't plunging into a new delirium. This was worse than the imaginary spiders I used to see in my drunken days because it sounded human. Or was I imagining it? In my condition, fighting claustrophobia and the heat, I was unable to tell reality from fantasy. The porthole at the end of the room finally faded from black to gray, and the night was over. I stumbled out on deck, aching with exhaustion.

The second night I approached my bunk apprehensively. Would I hear those sounds again? And if I did, could I hold on to my sanity? Perhaps it was already slipping. I crawled into the bed, the sheets already hot, and stretched out my nerve-wracked body to wait.

For some time the black, suffocating room was full of the sounds of two dozen women seeking sleep—tossing, coughing, sighing. Then a few gentle snores from those who had achieved the blessed state. Nothing else. The long night stretched before me. How many hours passed I don't know, but suddenly I sat up in my bunk, every nerve in my body tight. It had come, the sharp little cry and now the whimpering. Was it real? I had to know.

I reached up to grab the arm of the woman in the bunk above me. "Did you hear that?" I demanded in a hoarse whisper.

"How can I help it?" she said peevishly. "How is a body supposed to sleep with that goin' on?"

With an inward sigh I relaxed a bit. At least it wasn't in my mind. "What is it?" I asked.

"That woman on the other side of the room, by the door. The one with the little girl. She slaps the child at night."

"My God, why?"

"How do I know why? Go ask her. And tell her to keep that kid quiet so we can get some sleep."

Easing myself out of the bunk I tiptoed across the cabin toward the sound. A ventilating grill was above the door and through it came a spattering of light from the hall. It fell across the bunk with the mother and child. They stared up at me, the child with a bloated, tear-stained face, the mother with an expression that was dark, withdrawn, and hostile.

[*91*]

"What are you doing to that child?" I demanded.

"You mind your own business," the mother snapped.

"You're hitting her. I heard her cry."

"She's been naughty. I got a right to spank my own kid without you sticking your nose into it."

"But you spanked her all night last night. A helpless little child. My God. . . ."

"You get out of here." She hissed the words at me and she looked quite mad.

I knew that if I stayed another minute I would attempt to take the child from her. Through my mind raced a vision of this woman and I grappling together in the black cabin, hitting each other, pulling hair, screaming. Maybe both of us were mad.

I stumbled back to my bunk, found my robe, and threw it around me to make my way out of the bowels of the ship and up to the bridge. I think it was the captain who was on duty, he had gold braid all over his hat. Anyway I appealed to him to stop the mother beating her child. As I told the story I saw him look at me closely and I realized I was not making a very good impression. My hair wild, my talk even wilder, he couldn't have put much store in what I said.

He replied courteously enough. "Madam, I have no authority to prevent a parent disciplining her child. And if I did try to stop every spanking aboard this ship, I'd have time for nothing else."

"But she's a sadist, torturing that child. Something's got to be done. Somebody's got to stop it."

"I'm sorry, Madam."

He started to turn away but I grabbed his sleeve. "Is there a minister or a rabbi or a priest aboard?"

"Go to the purser's office. He can give you that information."

An hour later, I returned to the cabin with a sleepy young minister in tow. I think he had some misgivings about the whole thing but he waited in the hall while I went into the dormitory, took the woman by the arm and dragged her out bodily to meet him. Then I crawled back into my bunk.

For a long time I could hear the rise and fall of their voices, her's hysterical, his calming, soothing. I never knew what he said to her but the cries and whimperings stopped for the rest of the voyage. I suspected she beat the child in the daytime.

But now a new torture began. It seemed that as soon as I conquered one, I began a search for another. Our dormitory was directly over the drive-shaft that turned the giant propeller, and all night my bunk vibrated with its throbbing, pulsating power. I couldn't escape it. Even with my fingers in my ears I heard it, felt it.

After a time I began to sing a song to myself: "Silent Night, Holy Night, All is calm, all is bright." Just that part of the song, over and over and over, as we crawled through the endless Pacific. Why that particular song? Perhaps it was a little prayer on my part. If it started as a prayer, it became a curse. It sang thin and monotonous in my head all night and all day too: "Silent Night, Holy Night" over and over, without a let-up. No matter what I did, I couldn't be free of it. It filled me with terror.

At this stage, I had been out of a mental institution less than two years. Was I doomed to return? That thought increased my panic and my secret torment, "Silent Night, Holy Night."

I didn't want to tell Burt about it. I didn't want to crush his dreams and hopes. He had worked so hard for me, I couldn't bring myself to destroy everything by giving him a glimpse into me. I was sure once the voyage was over and we were on land, I'd be all right.

When we finally got to California I stepped ashore eagerly, prayerfully, but the secret sounds came ashore with me. "Silent Night" was grooved into my brain, and as the days passed I began to lose confidence, to think I'd never be really well mentally.

Burt was a dynamo of energy, getting new song arrangements, making dates for dress fittings, finding an accompanist to rehearse with me, haunting the offices of the booking agents. And all the time I clutched only at the edge of reality, "Silent Night" pushing me, pushing me over the brink.

Each day when Burt came home from his rounds of the booking agents he put on his boyish smile and said,

"Something's going to break for us real soon." But I knew the truth, he was getting the old brush-off. Lillian Roth was a has-been and nobody wanted her. It was worse than Burt knew—Lillian Roth was not only a has-been, she was about to fall apart completely.

The night came when I could suppress it no longer. I couldn't face it alone for another moment. I blurted everything out to Burt, hysteria mounting as the words tumbled and spilled. Burt showed no alarm, he appeared perfectly calm and assured. He sat me on the bed, took my hand and held it hard. He said, "Just stop everything now for a moment. Stop talking. Stop thinking. Stop breathing for a moment."

I took a long breath and held it, trying to clear my mind, to make it blank. Slowly I exhaled.

Burt said, "It will pass. It's always passed. Just be quiet . . . quiet."

After a few moments he reached for the Bible and began to read: "Thou shalt not be afraid of the terror by night, nor for the arrow that flieth by day."

And it passed, just as Burt had said, it passed away. How wrong it had been to conceal it all those weeks, for I had not the strength to surmount it alone. Once Burt shared the burden, it passed away.

I renewed work on *I'll Cry Tomorrow* which I had started in Australia. But the book was no answer to our immediate problems, either financial or emotional. I had to go back to work to save myself. I had to get bookings.

But nobody was interested in Lillian Roth. We hadn't made much money in Australia, and hadn't been able to take out of the country all we had made. Soon we were down to our last hundred dollars.

One evening, I found Burt reading the want ads. I knew that he had been doing this for about a week but concealing it from me because he was afraid I would think it meant surrender, a loss of faith. The truth was I needed Burt desperately to be my manager, my buffer, and if he had to get another job it would certainly mean a setback in our plans. But on the other hand, we were so far back already we could hardly be set back any farther, and we were just about broke. He was doing the sensible thing, as usual.

When I caught him with the want ads, he grinned sheepishly and said, "If we got a booking next week we wouldn't have the money for new arrangements or a gown. I thought I'd just lay us in a backlog of a few dollars."

"And besides, the rent is overdue," I smiled. He had tried to keep that fact from me.

"Oh yes, that," he said casually. "I'm a good salesman and there ought to be something I could sell here in the Los Angeles area. Hey, listen to this ad! 'If you are a salesman accustomed to $300 a week, if you are one who will not settle for less, you're our man. Call Mr. Knowlton for an appointment, MOnument 5-6400.'" Burt looked up

In June, 1954, just before the publication of *I'll Cry Tomorrow*, I "played the Palace," the one theatre in the world that spells success in showbusiness.

Jackie Gleason, the comedy team of Smith and Dale, and my sister Ann help me "cut a cake" in the lobby of the Palace as part of the Anniversary Celebration.

In 1955 M.G.M. bought *I'll Cry Tomorrow* for the screen. Here M.G.M.'s then studio head Dore Schary and I read the script for possible changes.

I'll Cry Tomorrow, starring Susan Hayward as Lillian Roth, opened in Hollywood in December, 1955. Eddie Fisher and Debbie Reynolds are among the hundreds of Hollywood luminaries who came to the screening.

Burt and I arrive at the theatre in Miami Beach, Florida for a home state screening of my picture in January, 1956.

Susan Hayward and I compare measurements. Susan's enactment of the Lillian Roth role won her a nomination for the Academy Award.

As I faced the war-shocked patients, the memories of my own mental illness came flooding back. But I sang and danced and brought off a double miracle . . . we had made each other whole.

As part of my act, I invite members of the audience to come up and dance with me. The show is completely successful only when audience and performer become one.

At home, between engagements,
I keep busy.

But there are moments
of relaxation . . .

. . . And an hour or two
for writing.

My wardrobe is constantly
supervised by me.

Of course I can make coffee!

Burt is a patient husband.

My three little friends are my constant companions. There are times when I have to "smuggle them," but they are always with me.

I give The Lip the benefit of my "lipmanship." Maurice Chevalier did the foreword for the French edition of my first book.

Making a record calls for meticulous attention. Sometimes you have to sing the same song over and over again to get it just right.

As I sing
I hope that this will be
the one they make.

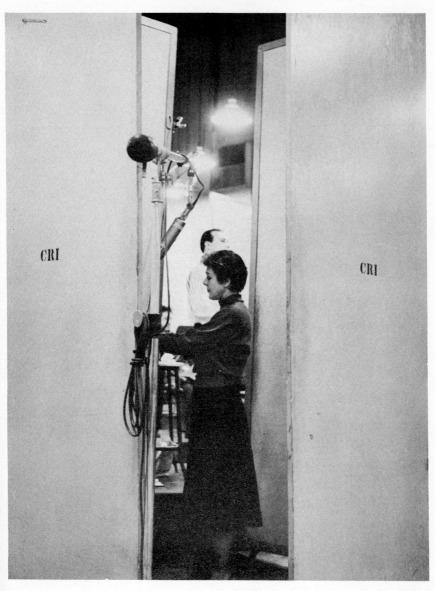

The high screens are used to catch every nuance of sound.

When I opened in Las Vegas,
Victor Mature came onstage to congratulate me.

Lili St. Cyr and I comprise
a double feature at *El Rancho*.

When the audience responded warmly to my performance
and I'd leave the stage in a storm of applause . . .

. . . my trip to the dressing room
would be like a journey on a cloud.

I have survived, I have grown stronger because of the people who came to me to receive help but ended by giving it. You have encouraged me and rewarded me with a credit beyond my worth.

at me wryly and said, "I'm a man who has settled for less, but I'm ready not to."

The next day Burt went for the interview while I stayed alone in the apartment and figured out what we would do with his first week's pay. We'd pay up the back rent, of course, and store some groceries, and then we wouldn't be so desperate about things and could catch our breath and take a calmer view of our situation. When Burt came home, however, he was not ebullient as when he left for the interview. Nor was he particularly depressed; he was thoughtful.

"Did you get it?" I demanded the moment he stepped into the room.

"Well, in a way. I have to let them know if I want it by the first of the week. It's selling strictly on commission. That three-hundred-dollar figure is something they just pulled out of the air. Still, I think I could make a go of it."

"Selling what, Burt?"

"Gumball machines."

"Selling what?"

"Those dispensing machines for gumballs you see in grocery stores and filling stations."

"My God!"

He shrugged his shoulders. "A lot of people chew gum. The shopkeeper gets a pretty good deal out of it and I think I could sell them. Here's the way it works: The merchant buys two of the machines for fifty dollars, with a twenty-dollar deposit. That deposit is my commission and I keep it. Also, I get twenty percent of the refill orders of gum during all the time the machines are in operation. They are serviced every month and all the merchant has to do is give it room in his store. Each salesman receives an exclusive territory so there is no competition to buck. They're offering me a territory that's never been worked."

"Where?" I asked.

"Highway sixty-six, all the way through Arizona and New Mexico and into Texas."

"They've given you the deserts," I cried.

He grinned. "Like I said, there won't be much competition."

"Are you going to do it, Burt?"

"Here's the way I've got it figured. We're not doing very well here in Hollywood and maybe we'll get the breaks faster back East. The gumball machines can pay our way. We'll hit a town, sell a couple of machines and make enough money to get us on to the next town. We'll have them chewing gumballs from here to New York."

So we went into the gumball business. There was a last-minute hitch when we discovered that we had to make an investment for the privilege of selling the merchandise; we had to buy two sample machines, one for the gum and one for peanuts. We sold our watches and a camera to raise the money.

The great highway unrolled before us, opportunity beckoning beyond each rise. The sales manager had said to us upon parting, "There isn't a town you'll hit that will have less than a half-dozen places needing these machines. Bars, grocery stores, filling stations, garages, bus terminals, hardware stores, they all need these machines. Why, you'll be rich by the time you get to New York."

Yes?

Well, let me tell you that until you have a gumball machine in the back of your car to sell, you don't realize how many of these contraptions already exist in the world! For the first two days of the trip every place we stopped already had one. It seemed the whole territory had already been "chewed up."

"We must be on the wrong road," Burt joked. "It wasn't supposed to be like this."

"We'll never make it to Phoenix at this rate," I said.

"Perhaps we should try the back roads, hit the rural areas. Surely they can't be loaded up with gumballs."

They weren't, but neither were they about to be. The first "town" we came to was a cluster of a half-dozen ancient, unpainted houses grouped around a general store at a hot, dusty crossroad. Burt braked the car to a stop before a half-dozen men in faded dungarees and with lean, hostile faces, who lounged on the store steps. Some were whittling, others sent small bombs of chewing tobacco juice into the dusty road from time to time, the rest just sat and stared at the parched horizon.

"One of those is my customer," Burt said under his breath. "Wish me luck."

"Good luck," I whispered.

He climbed from behind the wheel and went to the back of the car to open the trunk and remove one of the sample machines. These machines were attached to an iron base and very heavy and difficult for Burt to manage. He couldn't walk with his cane when he carried one because he had to wrap both his good arm and his bad arm around the glass bowl in order to lift it. Apprehensively I watched him make his way toward the men, half-carrying and half-dragging the machine. And then it happened! He fell.

With a small cry I started to climb out of the car but he raised himself on one elbow and glared at me, forcing me back into the car. He was determined to do this on his own. Without his cane, it was difficult for him to get to his feet, and the first time he tried he lost his balance and fell back down into the dust. He lay there a moment, panting. Not a man on the steps moved to help him. My throat ached with pity and anger.

On the second attempt he made it to his feet, got the machine erect and dragged it the rest of the way to the store. Slowly and carefully he dusted himself off and then said, "Which of you gentlemen owns this store?" The owner identified himself by spitting into the dust at Burt's feet. Burt said, "I have a machine here, sir, that will make you a tidy sum of money each month and with no effort on your part beyond giving it a place to stand."

He went on with his sales presentation, talking animatedly, earnestly, but not a man on the steps changed expression. Six faces looked at him impassively, but no, there was an expression there and it chilled me: There was suspicion and cruelty on the thin lips. We were strangers and they did not trust us.

When Burt finally finished his sales pitch, the owner of the store said, "I don't want none of them new-fangled things."

Burt started to repeat some of the sales talk. The man shifted from one haunch to the other and though the movement was slow, almost casual, it was full of violence. He said in a flat voice, "Mister, you better git!"

I jumped out and ran to Burt, and together we dragged the gumball machine back to the car and drove off.

All that day it was the same, as was the next and the next, through the back roads of Arizona, New Mexico, and Texas. Not only were these farmers and store owners suspicious of strangers, and doubly suspicious of Yankees, but Burt made the worst impression of all. Due to the polio attack in his childhood he hadn't been able to speak until he was nine years old, and then he had been taught diction by an English governess. So today his speech is very crisp and cultured. It must have fallen on the ears of those hillbilly farmers with a most unpleasing effect; it certainly raised their hackles in no time flat.

My heart ached for Burt during those hot and merciless days. All I could see was this charming boy with his wonderful education and his fine mind but a poor right leg and right arm, too weak to carry properly these terrible gumball machines, and the humiliation he had to endure every time we stopped the car in front of a country store.

Sometimes, in the late afternoon, when he'd stagger back to the car with the machine, he'd drop into the front seat and weep from exhaustion and frustration. And then I'd weep too. But finally we would stop weeping and laugh at ourselves and drive on, only to another defeat and perhaps to more tears, but always with hope.

We got as far as Dallas and then our money ran out. We had sold a total of two machines in a trip through four states, not enough to pay for our gas, let alone food and shelter. Now we were at our lowest ebb. We had twenty-five dollars left, and the car. Oh yes, and a back seat full of gumballs. But we had learned there isn't much nourishment in them. One thing we had done when we left California, we had arranged with an agent, an old friend of mine, Lou Irwin, that he should send a wire to us in care of the automobile club in Dallas in case anything opened up. Providentially, there was a wire!

Lou, bless him, had booked me into the "Blue Room" of the New Orleans Hotel for a month, at what seemed to me then the miraculous sum of seven hundred and fifty dollars a week. Burt and I made the distance to New Orleans on our twenty-five dollars, plus the part-refund from the machines we turned in. I had saved three or four of my gowns and had them with me. We swept into the hotel as if I was *the* Lillian Roth and had never heard of gumballs.

After New Orleans, we got a week's booking in a New

Jersey hotel and it began to look as if things were rolling. But again there was a setback. After my first show, the manager came and looked me up and down and said, "Miss Roth, I'm sorry I booked you."

"Why?"

"Well, I don't like your act."

"That is your privilege, of course. But if you tell me exactly what you don't like, maybe I can change it."

He shook his head. "It's nothing I can put my finger on. I just think it's vulgar."

This was a great shock to me. For a moment I couldn't think of anything to say. I opened and closed my mouth several times and finally came out with, "You must be joking."

"Why must I be joking?"

"Because I . . . I've never used any blue material in my life."

"It's not a question of your material, there's nothing much wrong with that, I guess."

"Then what?" I demanded.

"I guess it's your personality. I don't like it."

By now I was beginning to burn and I said, "I'm very sorry but there's not much I can do about that, is there?"

"Well, don't get lippy."

It was clear to me now that he was determined to pick a fight. And I was determined not to give it to him.

He put his nose close to mine and sneered, "You're nothing but a lush. I don't care how long you've been off the stuff, you'll go back to it. They all do. Helen Morgan worked for me once, and I know."

I turned and walked away from him, sickened. It wasn't only his attack upon me that made me feel that way, but that someone like him should sneer at Helen Morgan, at a wonderful woman who could no longer defend herself.

Back in my hotel room I felt greatly depressed. Helen Morgan—what a tragedy. I had known her only casually, but I had once hoped to follow in her footsteps. And I almost did, right to the bitter end.

I first worked the same bill with Helen at the Old Amsterdam, on Broadway, in 1929, just before I went into pictures. What a wonderful old theater-restaurant that was, how full of memories. It seated about a thousand people. The Ziegfeld Theater was in the same building, and people who came to the Ziegfeld would see the play and then take the elevator up to the roof for our night-club performances. Paul Whiteman and his orchestra, with the Rhythm Boys, one of whom was Bing Crosby, were among the steadies. I remember that Ziegfeld never thought any of the Rhythm Boys would go very far. Ted Husing was Master of Ceremonies and each evening he'd announce the "most beautiful girls in the world."

Every two weeks new stars were added to the show and I remember watching from the wings as they performed— Gladys Glad, Mark Hellenger's wife, the wonderful Ruth Etting, the Duncan Sisters, Maurice Chevalier, and Helen Morgan! I felt a great kinship toward Helen. Not that I

could ever hope to have her beauty, but I think I felt some
of the loneliness and ache that was in her.

She was already drinking heavily when I first knew her
and sometimes she'd take me, a young kid, into her dressing room and say, "Lillian darling, don't ever do to yourself what I'm doing." Ah, if I had only listened to her. If I
had only understood that she knew she couldn't help herself but that she wanted to help someone, wanted to help
me.

Over the years she drank more and more, sometimes to
the point where she couldn't go on. I often substituted for
her at such moments. She'd say, "Send for Lillian," and
I'd take her place on stage.

When I went to Hollywood, our paths separated. But
they came together again one evening in the late 1930's,
when we did a benefit show together. When she saw me
back-stage, she ran over and embraced me, holding me
close, warm and affectionate. But there seemed a hidden
frenzy about her and when she finally spoke it was with a
little laugh that was half a sob. She said, "Lillian, I'm so
glad to see you. Darling, guess what? I'm dying. I'll be gone
within two years."

"Oh Helen!" I cried. "How can you talk like that!" I
gazed into her exquisite face, etched as fine as a cameo, yet
so alive, and I thought that this loveliness couldn't be gone
in two years. It just couldn't. Yet, even as I looked at her I
seemed to see a shadow behind her eyes, a half-glimpsed
cloud that moved fleetingly. I saw that look again later in

my mother's eyes, just before she died. It was like a cold hand on my heart, but I put on an act. I ruffled her hair and said, "Helen, how could you be up and running around like this if that was true? Why, it's ridiculous."

"No darling, I'm serious," she said. "The doctor said the lining of my tummy is gone. And if I can't sing I don't want to live."

"Shouldn't you be in bed?" I asked.

She shook her tousled head. "I've got to hear music. I've got to be where there's life . . ."

At this moment, the stage manager called, "Helen, you're on!"

She turned and walked out onto the stage and took her famous position atop a grand piano. The stage darkened and a single spot picked up her delicate face to frame it while her sweet, throbbing, heartbreaking voice sang, "Why was I born . . . why am I living . . . what do I get . . . what am I giving."

My throat closed and my eyes swam with tears.

The last time I saw Helen was in the very week she died. She was playing the Chicago Theater, and I was in Chicago singing at a small club. I was by now on the steep road down and drinking heavily. Ill as she was, she searched me out, took my hands in hers and said, "Baby, baby, look what you're doing to yourself. Please stop drinking. Please."

That weekend she was dead. And I, who had often

taken her place on stage, who took her place in an alcoholic whirl, almost followed her to the grave.

Now, after all those years, I still felt pain when anyone made a slurring remark about Helen Morgan. This hotel manager who disliked my personality, well, I could take that because I never claimed to have a lovable personality for everyone, but I was mad about his sneers at Helen. When Burt came into the room, I told him I wanted to quit the engagement, and why.

He thought about it calmly, as he always did when I rushed into things, and then said, "You know there are a lot of reasons why you shouldn't quit any engagement right now."

"A lot of personal reasons, career reasons, sure," I said. "But sometimes a loyalty to a friend. . . ."

Burt raised his hand to stop me. "Let me ask you one question, Lillian. If Helen had been the performer here, and if this man had called her a lush, what would she have done? Would she have quit or gone on stage?"

"She would have gone on," I said in a low voice.

And that was that. I had to try and do as well as my idol.

On the long comeback road, during all that happened, Burt and I always shared our burdens and problems, propping each other up, comforting each other when we fell. That became the close and tender part of us. One night, I was feeling badly about my physical condition. I had re-

ceived such beatings and kickings from a previous husband, and had undergone a terrible operation, which
made me unable to bear children. I was feeling guilty
about this and wondering if Burt wouldn't one day resent
my barrenness. "I'm only half a woman," I said bitterly.
"I'm nothing but a shell."

"*You're* nothing but a shell," he scoffed. "Me, with my
bad arm and bad leg, how do you feel about me?"

How did I feel about him? I loved him. His physical
disabilities had nothing to do with my love. If man was
made in God's image, then this likeness is man's inner
formation, not his imperfect body. And inside of us is sadness, and that is Godly too, I think.

5

Success and Sorrow

Burt and I were never again as broke as during that trip through the Southwest with the gumball machines. We were to have more years of struggle to get decent bookings, but that was the last time we actually wondered where our next meal was coming from.

The engagement at the New Orleans Hotel in 1948 gave us enough of a grubstake in both money and self-confidence to allow us to strike out for the larger cities in the East. It was a long and tough road, and, as I already mentioned, the first important break, the first booking into a quality New York club did not come until late in 1953, when I played *La Vie en Rose*. And as so often happens in this life, as soon as success was achieved in one direction, opportunities seemed to open in several.

One evening, a talent scout named Bob Theile arrived

with Don Cornell to catch my show at *La Vie,* and afterwards came backstage to say, "I want you to make some
recordings for Coral Records."

"Me?" I said, laughing at him.

"Sure. Why not?"

"Mr. Theile, I don't have a record voice and you know
it." I thought he was kidding me and I was making darn
sure I wasn't taken in. In my type of singing before live
audiences I don't worry about forming perfect vowels and
perfect phrasing. If I need a smile or a giggle to get over
a point to the audience, well, I just sacrifice sound for
lyric. I just didn't have the smoothness for records, I was
sure.

"Lillian, I'm perfectly serious," he insisted. "I've listened to you carefully and I know you'll record well. Anyway, come on over to the studio next Monday afternoon
and let's cut a platter. I'm sure it will be good."

When he left my dressing room I tried to calm the but-
terflies in my stomach. I had always wanted to make
records, but during the years I was with Paramount my
contract prevented me from doing it and, of course, during my illness I was unable.

I was thrilled, but I was nervous too. The truth was, I
still feared people and lacked confidence in myself. I knew
I had so much to learn after all those lost years of alcoholism, my life consisted of one faltering step after another
and I was never quite sure that I'd make the journey. I
was now forty-one years old and if I lost my equilibrium

and fell, it might be too much for me to rise and start over again.

I was beginning to make my way in the night clubs, why take a chance on records, something I had never done before? Late that night, however, after talking it over with Burt, I defeated my caution and my misgivings and decided to make the record.

Monday noon I woke up feeling terrible. I had a bad cold and 102 degrees temperature. I thought to myself, is this psychosomatic? Did I catch this cold just so I could avoid the recording date this afternoon? Now I had a legitimate excuse not to put myself to the test; all I had to do was stay in bed under doctor's orders. But did I want to? Did I dare? At a moment like this in the old days I would have reached for a bottle of whiskey to solve my problem. I was grateful that *this* solution to my anxieties did not seriously present itself. At least I'd come this far. But I still had to prove myself.

At the studio my cold was so bad I could hardly hear myself. But the recording officials said, "Well, let's make a test record, anyway." So we went through a few rehearsals and then I stepped up in front of the microphone and started to sing. The people in the control room nodded through the glass and gave me the sign that everything was fine. After the first break, everybody swarmed around me and said I was just great—a new, husky voice, a voice with a gimmick they called it. When they played the recording back to me I didn't recognize my own voice at first. I thought it sounded hoarse and strange. But the producers and the technicians liked it and we cut the entire album.

The record—gimmick or no gimmick—wasn't too successful. Since I am my own toughest critic, and somewhat of a perfectionist, I had mixed feelings about the record all along and whenever I was a guest on a disk-jockey show and the discussion came around to my own recording, I'd give my frank opinion.

One jockey laughed and said on the air, "Ladies and gentlemen, this is the very first time in my experience that I've heard a recording star get on the air and run down her own recordings."

"I'm not running them down that far," I said, "I just don't think they are as good as they should have been and I think I have a responsibility to my public to say so. Not everyone in a different field of show business has mastered the art of recording, and I'm one who hasn't. I'm not being unduly modest. Matter of fact, I think that a lot of recording artists probably haven't mastered a stage performance the way I have."

"Well, tell me, Lillian," the disk jockey said, "who is your favorite recording star?"

"Oh, I don't know that I have any one favorite. Certainly Frankie Laine has a wonderfully exciting delivery. And I think Nat Cole is splendid. And then there's Toni Arden; I don't think anyone sells a ballad better than she does on recordings. But Lillian Roth, well, she's definitely *not* one of my favorite recording artists. Not yet. Maybe someday, but not yet."

I didn't cut another record for three years. Then I signed to make an album for Epic, a subsidiary of Decca Records.

A funny thing happened, too: On recording day I came down with a cold. By now I was certain that my colds were psychosomatic. But I had already told the Epic people about my cold on the Coral album so I couldn't very well come up with this one again. Though true, it would seem to be a standard excuse. I just had to go through with the songs. It turned out pretty good. What helped greatly was the fact that I now had a much larger measure of self-confidence than at the previous time I recorded. I said to myself: Now look here, that's just a little old microphone hanging in front of you and it's not going to bite you. You just make believe there are a lot of people behind it, seated at tables and having a good time; pretend this is not going just into a microphone but out to a lot of people to listen to and enjoy.

Also, I had asked that this time I be allowed to add little thoughts and sayings between each song in an effort to make it intimate, as if the listener and I were old friends and just talking things over. This helped me to establish a feeling of contact with that great unseen audience.

And certainly the biggest help I got was from the orchestra leader, Don Costa. To achieve the proper balance between voice and orchestra, a screen had been put around me and my mike, but Don stood on a box to look over the screen at me while he conducted the orchestra. There was that round, disembodied head looking at me with a most reassuring smile. I thought that if everybody was enjoying themselves as much as Don, I must be doing all right. He gave me confidence and I was deeply grateful to him.

The album had twelve sides and was entitled "I'll Cry Tomorrow." After it had been released, the Epic people told me that it was one of the best selling albums of their 1956 season.

My third venture into recordings occurred in 1957. I wanted to make an album that my teen-age fans could afford. The price of $3.95 on my Epic records prevented a lot of young people from buying them. So I signed with Tops Records, a concern that distributes through drug stores and supermarkets at a more reasonable price. This time I sang only those tunes I'd always sung to myself, the kind that made me cry a little or smile a little when I was lonely or carried a torch. Sometimes they made me feel even sadder and more lonely, yet I hum them anyway because they touch something deep within me.

I sang "Until the Real Thing Comes Along," and did it in a real tender style: "I'd work for you, I'd slave for you, I'd be a beggar or a knave for you . . ." Bobby Kroll and I wrote a theme song called "Beyond My Worth," and we recorded that. Then we did, "You Must Have Been a

Beautiful Baby." I was a little wary of that one because I had had some trouble remembering the arrangement at the end. Bobby had said, "Okay, take this high note and then you'll be sure to remember it." He struck it on the piano and I listened, then we recorded the song from the beginning, accompanied by a small jazz combo.

I took the song in swingy tempo and suddenly found myself elaborating it with counter melody. When I came to the finish I went up an octave, higher than I had ever gone before in my life and right on pitch. That one rehearsal was the take. I was astounded because I had been completely free and easy. I hadn't done a thing wrong. And I didn't have a cold!

Before I ever heard the completed record I felt it was a personal success, for me, anyway, because I had overcome so many fears and had learned so many new things in order to do it to my satisfaction. This kind of confidence comes with time, with age. When you're young you're afraid to take a chance at new things, but as you get older you think, "Gee, here's an opportunity to try something new and I can't pass it by because there won't be too many more chances in this life. I'll just do it the best I can and it might come out right. If it doesn't, well, it's not going to weigh too much in the scales against me . . ."

Sometimes, after you've worked hard for many, many years without seeing any progress, all the breaks seem to come at once; success cascades over you like a waterfall until you lose your breath and cry out, "Not so fast! Dear Lord, not so fast!" I wanted all this, but a little at a time so I'd know and feel what was happening, savor the wonderment.

That was the way I felt in the summer of 1954. Night club offers poured in from all over the country; my book was a best seller, and then the movies wanted to film my life story!

My first reaction was, oh no! I thought I was going to be able to close the book on that part of my life. I felt that by now I had earned the right to be accepted on my professional ability alone. I wouldn't want my life acted out and filmed and projected on movie screens all over the world. This was illogical, of course, as I soon realized. If I had revealed all the intimate things about me in a book because I thought it would serve a good purpose, then why draw the line at the movies? If I had a message, and I thought I did, I should want it given the widest possible circulation. There was no logical reason for me to refuse to let the motion picture people have the story.

After the book came out, almost every studio in Hollywood wanted the story. But, at an earlier date, I had given MGM a verbal option and I held to my word. Also, they had promised that Susan Hayward would be given the title role, as I had requested. I had followed her career and thought she was an extremely skilled and sensitive actress. So, I turned down the other offers and notified MGM I was ready to sign a contract.

I met Susan Hayward first in Las Vegas, where I was working, and she came to see my performance several times. About a month later, she visited me again at the Beverly Hills Hotel in Hollywood. It was in the early afternoon and she arrived in her black Chinese pajamas with a coat thrown over them. We talked for several hours. By the time she left, I didn't know whether she was imitating me or I was emulating her. We were both so emotional about things that when we faced each other it was almost like looking into a mirror; I was looking at Lillian and she was looking at Susan.

I thought I knew Susan intimately. My sense of identification with her was so great, that a few months later when the newspapers were full of black headlines about her attempted suicide during the filming of the picture, I knew exactly what had happened. Susan never told me the facts about that episode, but I'm sure I know them because she has the same intense emotional make-up I have.

The lurid newspaper stories reported that Susan had been studying the movie script of *I'll Cry Tomorrow* late into the night, became so terribly depressed over the story that she attempted suicide with an overdose of sleeping pills. In any event she was rushed to the hospital where her stomach was pumped out and her life saved. There were gossip magazines that claimed Susan had been determined to marry Howard Hughes but that he jilted her that day and she didn't want to live any longer.

I don't believe Susan intended to commit suicide at all;

she is too vital and eager, too ambitious a girl to want to end her life. No, I think she was probably highly nervous during the filming of the picture and that night while reading the script she might have had a few cocktails and then, being very tired and knowing she had to work in the morning, took some sleeping pills. The alcohol and the sleeping pills fought each other, slowing her pulse, making her respiration extremely shallow, lowering her skin temperature. When your nerves are a little off the beam, this can happen to you; it happened to me.

I remember one time when I was drinking heavily, I thought that if I took some sleeping pills I'd be able to sleep it off. The next thing I knew it was early in the morning and someone was shaking me, slapping me, and shoving fingers down my throat. It was a woman, an old friend of my mother, who had just happened to find me in this comatose condition. She was a nurse and had been giving me artificial respiration for over an hour.

She explained to me that if you take sleeping pills over a period, the narcotic begins to accumulate at the base of the brain and when combined with alcohol depresses your respiration until you have hardly any breath. After that experience I had the horrors and jitters for a long time and was careful not to combine alcohol with those little dream tablets.

That's what I think happened to Susan. There were articles that hinted she did it on purpose to study how I felt, to follow my footsteps. But who would ever want to follow in my alcoholic footsteps?

After signing the picture contracts, the studio suggested that I continue my night-club work because it was good promotion for the film. I set out on another cross-country tour and was never near Hollywood during the actual filming of my life.

The first time I saw the picture was at a special press preview in Chicago. I was very nervous when I went. I had no idea of what the studio might have done with my life. I was to sit with the reporters and the critics and I knew they'd be watching my reactions. I prayed I wouldn't show any emotion at all. Still, I felt those little palpitations in my heart, my mouth was dry, and the palms of my hands damp. Do I have to see all the horrors of my life on the screen, I wondered. How do I get myself into these situations? How can I get out of this? There was no escape. My jaw began to tighten. I fought against the return of the old symptoms. The small preview theater darkened and the screen came alive.

As the story unfolded, I tried to be objective about it, tried to view it not as my life but as a story about some other person. Susan's performance was magnificent. My throat tightened as I suffered with her. I began to fill up with tears. I wiped them away quickly, hoping none of the newspaper men would notice.

But I lost emotional control the moment my mother—

played by Jo Van Fleet—appeared on the scene. It broke my heart to see, to relive, the terrible things I did to her, the way I made her suffer. I could feel myself gagging and the tears spilled over but I was too embarrassed to reach for a handkerchief.

I thought Jo Van Fleet did a fine job though she was directed to play the part in a way that was not quite true to fact. In the picture, my mother spoke with a foreign accent, whereas she was actually born in Boston and justifiably proud of her speech. There is nothing wrong with a foreign accent, our ancestors were all immigrants, but it was just wasn't the way my mother spoke. Nor did she go around in furs and jewels. She was always neatly and modestly dressed, not at all an extrovert.

As my life progressed there on the screen, it became impossible for me to watch and I just closed my eyes. When the lights went up at the end of the picture it took me some time to recover my speech.

When I did, I went to a telephone to call Hollywood and tell Susan what a wonderful job she had done. She was very pleased. I even congratulated her on the singing and said, "Susie—you are stealing my line, eh?" She laughed and I slowly regained my composure.

It was necessary for me to see the picture a second time, at the big Hollywood premier. I went with Susan, her escort, and my husband. I told myself that this time I mustn't cry because it would look as if I was sorry for myself. I certainly didn't want all the picture people to think I was weak and full of self-pity. No, this time I really would look at it as if it were the story of some other person.

Oh, I was brave all right. Tears flowed more freely this time than before. Out of the corner of my eye I saw that tears were running down Susan's cheeks too. She wasn't weeping for me, or for the character up there on the screen, I believe, but for some other deep ache inside her that the picture seemed to touch. Then everybody in the audience was crying and so I don't suppose they noticed my tears at all. All the big he-men began to cough and blow their noses hard, as if they had colds. It was a real weepy evening.

I said to Burt later that night, "I'm never going to see that picture again. It takes too much out of me."

It has taken time for me to obtain perspective about the picture. Perhaps I haven't yet achieved it completely, because, after all, it is my life and one can hardly be objective in such a case. But I think one big factor in the book and in my life was missing in the picture: my search to know God, to please Him, and love Him, which had saved me from self-destruction.

However, I think many people went away from the picture with a new consciousness of the responsibility they must bear for their own actions. Without being preachy, or unduly melodramatic, the picture warned of the tragedy and suffering of alcoholism and it showed that it is possible, with God's help, to overcome any problem.

For that I will ever be grateful.

6

And He Walks With Me . . .

After the release of the movie, in November 1955, my mail tripled and it took my secretary and me long hours every day to keep abreast of it. I feel duty-bound to read every letter I receive because I honestly believe that if a person takes the time and trouble to write to me, the least I can do is to give him the courtesy his interest deserves. Whenever possible, I sent out a word of encouragement to those in trouble for even though I didn't think I was going to solve anyone's problem, I knew from experience what a kind word can mean at a time of darkness.

During the next few weeks two letters arrived amidst the avalanche of mail which were to leave a particularly lasting impression on me. One was from an old people's home in upper New York State, the other from a prisoner in California. The letter from the old people's home was a more or less routine invitation to come and entertain the residents. I receive dozens of such invitations every week and can't possibly accept them all. But in this particular case I was going to play a club engagement nearby and so I wrote and told them to expect me on a Monday night, when I would have an evening free.

When I arrived at the home, I found I wasn't the only entertainer. The Mariners, a quartet of two white and two Negro singers who used to appear regularly on the Arthur Godfrey shows, were also present. I had watched them often on TV and not only admired their musicianship but also the wholesome, straightforward, unprejudiced way they worked together. I was delighted to appear on a program with them.

This particular "home" was anything but homelike; it had a bleak, antiseptic, institutional atmosphere, and the Mariners and I determined to try and make the residents forget their surroundings for a while. We met in the "social room," a narrow, high-ceilinged room, painted a scabrous yellow, and illuminated by the pale wash of a half-dozen naked light bulbs. But when the Mariners burst out in full-throated song, all of us forgot the room and gave ourselves over to the joy of their music.

Following their program, the Mariners asked for requests from the audience and at once there rose a thin, old voice saying, "Please sirs, I'd truly like to hear 'In the Garden.'" The bass of the quartet replied, "We don't have that music with us and I'm afraid we can't remember the lyrics without it."

Other requests began to be called out but something made that Mariner take a few steps to the side of the room to see the face of the person who had asked for "In the Garden." It was an elderly Negro lady, her eyes milky with cataracts. A fleeting expression passed over that young Negro singer's face; pity and compassion, yes. But also other things, too deep and complicated for me to interpret. He turned back to the rest of the quartet and called out, "Boys, we gotta sing 'In the Garden.' If we forget the words we just hum it, and if we forget the tune we can keep time with our hands."

They sang the song with rich and reverent voices, forgetting some of the words, true, but remembering the important ones: "And He walks with me and He talks with me and He tells me I am His own . . ."

As they sang, the old lady leaned her head on the back of her chair, a gentle smile on her lips and in her sightless eyes.

I sang a few songs after the Mariners and then asked if I might visit the wards to talk with those too infirm to come to the social room. Permission was granted and I began a tour of the building, talking to perhaps a dozen bed-ridden old people with faces that reflected both the pain and the beauty of life. At the end of one of the halls there was a private room and I was told that in there an old woman was dying. I asked permission to visit her.

In the darkened room I saw a white face on the white pillow and for a moment I thought death had arrived ahead of me, but then she opened her dark eyes and there was life enough in them—they fairly sparked with hostility.

Her first words, after being introduced, were, "What's a woman like you doing here?"

"Well, I . . ."

"Curious! That's it. Want to see what an old crone looks like!"

I shook my head.

"I came here because I like elderly women. I think they are wise and beautiful. And, most important, they remind me of my mother who is gone."

She looked at me with her bird-quick eyes and said, "But I've never been a mother."

I looked straight back at her and said, "Neither have I." Then I waited to see how she'd react. A change came over her face, it softened and even saddened a bit. I knew I had touched her and so I hastened to say, "So you see, we have something in common. And don't you see, we're not wasted just because we're not mothers, look at all the motherless people we can give our love to. There are so many lonely people who need us."

Then her dry, brittle old hand reached toward me and I took it in mine. Her expression softened and there was none of the resentment and anger left which had greeted me.

When we drove away from that state institution, I felt

there was so much to be done to brighten the days of these old people. If we all would only give a little bit of our love and affection we could realize the truth of the Christopher Movement's saying, "You can change the world."

The letter from the prisoner in California arrived about a week after my visit to the old people's home. It led to a very unusual experience. It read:

"Dear Miss Roth: For many many months now I have been trying to get up enough courage to write this letter. My name is Eugene Emery Logan and I'm an inmate at the Soledad State Prison at Soledad, California. You have never met me, though I met you in the pages of your book, *I'll Cry Tomorrow*. I am serving a life sentence here at the prison for a tragedy that occurred between me and my wife in August of 1953. Many many months back my family sent me the story of your life as a birthday present and I read it from the beginning to end on the night I received it. Never before have I been so moved by the life story of another person.

"I saw that you and I had a lot in common, not the same problem, but a heart filled with sorrow. I was so moved that when I finished reading your book I wrote a song, the first song I'd ever written. It was done after the lights were out and everything was quiet in the prison.

"I thought the song was good so I kept writing, and since then have completed over two hundred songs and all because of reading your story. When I saw how you faced your hardships, I knew that I could also face mine. I have a completely new outlook on life now, the future has become worth living. If my wife, whose life I took, were alive today she'd be proud of what I am doing, just as my six-year-old son will someday be proud.

"This letter is no sales pitch, for I have nothing to sell you, I just want you to know the wonderful thing your story has done for me. I want to give the world some beautiful songs, not money-making songs but songs with feeling and depth. Money can do me no good here, for there is nothing I can ever spend it on. (Signed) Eugene Emery Logan."

There was something about this letter, something between the lines perhaps, that touched me and I wrote him a long one in reply. He wrote back at once and sent me some of his songs.

I must say here that I receive a lot of songs from amateur songwriters and there is very little I can do about them except return them or file them away. It would be physically impossible for me to arrange for the publication of all of them or even evaluate them. I hope all the songwriters who have sent me material will understand my position.

Now that I've made the above statement I have to reveal that in Eugene Logan's case I *did* pay attention to his songs. I can only explain it by saying that in his case I felt some sort of cry I couldn't ignore. So I read his songs carefully and then had my accompanist play them for me. I was amazed, for here was this prisoner's first contact with music, he was completely untutored, yet there was a spirituality about his work.

Oh, I know he was a murderer, but that didn't mean he was without spirituality, or that God had deserted him. He had killed another human being and thereby committed a crime against God and man; yet, who knew what demons rode him at that moment, or what remorse had wracked him since? It is God's province to judge his crime, not man's.

Certainly I was not without sin and my life, being what it was, gave me a greater capacity to understand him, to know there could have been extenuating circumstances. He said that I already had helped him through my book, and that made me feel very good. I wrote and told him I hoped he'd continue to write songs because there was beauty to bring to the world.

This started up a correspondence that has lasted to this day. I don't exactly know why it happened, there just seemed to be a compulsion on both our parts to share our thoughts and emotions. In one letter he wrote, "If you're ever out this way, the boys and I wish you'd drop in for a visit."

I did just that six months later.

I was in San Francisco and said to Lloyd Johnson, a newspaper friend of mine, "Lloyd, do you know anybody at Soledad prison?"

"I got a few friends there for varying terms," he quipped.

"I'm serious. I've been corresponding with a prisoner there and I'd like to visit him."

Within a matter of minutes Lloyd had the warden on the phone. I said, "I'd be happy to try and entertain the boys if I can come to see Eugene. It's not much of a contribution but I can sing a few songs and maybe brighten their day a bit."

"Come along and welcome," the warden said.

Two days later Lloyd and Bobby Kroll and I set out on the one-hundred-fifty-mile trip to Soledad prison. As we came upon it I was surprised, for I found that everything was very bright and modern. The prison was a two-story brick building that wanders among lawns and flower beds, and might be a middle income apartment house if you didn't look closely enough to see the bars at the windows.

The warden, a tall, fine-looking and friendly man, met me and escorted me into a small foyer which held samples of the prisoners' work for sale. There were leather goods tooled in intricate designs and the warden displayed them with great pride. I learned later that this was not just an ordinary prison but a very progressive one that put emphasis upon rehabilitation of the inmates.

A lunch had been laid out for us in a small dining room and though I wasn't the least bit hungry there seemed no way of avoiding it without hurt feelings. I sat down and the trustees who acted as waiters hovered over me anticipating my enjoyment of every bite.

"How is it, Miss Roth?" one of them asked eagerly.

"Very good," I said.

"Hey, I'll tell Andy in the kitchen. He cooked it especially for you."

"You give Andy my compliments and my thanks," I said.

They were like housewives who had slaved over hot stoves for important guests and wanted so terribly to have the meal a success. I actually relished the food because of the pleasure it gave them.

Seated at my left was the prison chaplain, a priest with merry eyes. He said, "The entire prison is excited over your visit. The boys have talked about nothing else since it was announced."

"I'll do my best to entertain them."

The warden spoke up. "Your message is very important, too."

"Message?" I exclaimed. "I don't want to preach at the men, I just want to lighten their load a bit if I can. Perhaps I have a couple of thoughts I can give them, but no heavy 'message' to depress them. How many will there be, Warden?"

"Well, that was a problem. We couldn't get the entire prison population into the recreation room so we thought and thought and finally decided you could be sponsored by one of the local prisoner organizations and then just members of that group would be eligible to come."

The priest leaned toward me with a twinkle in his

eyes. "Our local chapter of Alcoholics Anonymous claimed you as their own and won out against all the others. So you're their guest."

"That's fine with me," I said. "How many do you have in A.A.?"

The warden laughed. "We had about fifty until your visit was announced. Overnight we got five hundred new members and then we had to stop the enrollment because we couldn't admit any more to your performance."

After lunch we started for the recreation hall and had to pass through the main cell block. For this occasion the cell doors had all been opened, allowing the prisoners to mill about. Now I'm not the bravest girl in the world, in fact I've sometimes found it difficult to walk down a dark city street at night, and lonely subways terrify me, yet here I had to move through a long, long corridor called "Main Street," and it was jammed with hundreds of inmates. Yet I was without fear. I had a strange feeling that we all understood each other and as I walked along I smiled and said "Hi" and wanted to reach out and shake hands with each one of them.

Every now and then one of them stepped forward to thrust out a copy of my book and ask for an autograph. Some younger ones gave me a big wink, which was real cute, considering my age, and I winked in reply. The chaplain told me later that I was the only woman ever to walk through the cell blocks when the men were not locked up. Those men treated me like I was a sister, or a best girl, and that trip through the cell block left me humble and glad.

When we arrived at the recreation hall, which looked more like a large classroom than anything else, we found close to five hundred men jammed into it. Across one end was a big banner with photographs of me pinned on it and hand-lettering that said, "Welcome Lillian Roth," and "Soledad Alcoholics Anonymous and Inmates Welcome Lillian."

The president and the secretary of the A.A. group came up to meet me and give me a bouquet of flowers that had been grown in the prison garden, then escorted me to the front of the room. As I walked down the center aisle I turned from right to left and tried to speak to all of them and thank them for the flowers and the reception.

The faces that were turned up to me: some old and beaten by life, some so tragically young with the hardness in them not yet set, where hope and despair still warred.

When I got to the front of the room I found an upright piano and a sort of stage, formed by separating my performing space from the audience by a barricade of heavy tables. I didn't like this feeling of separation and I asked for volunteers to shove the tables aside so we could be all together. The men responded with a cheer and the tables were whisked aside as if they weighed nothing. There had been a tension in the room but now it eased and there were broad smiles on the faces.

Then I stood up there and just looked at the men for a few moments and they looked back at me with a hushed expectancy. I didn't know what I was going to say to them. I never plan my talks, and when the words came they seemed entirely unbidden. I feel it is difficult to be sincere if you prepare your speech in advance. Unless you are on the scene and can gauge the audience and the circumstances your prepared words often seem out of place. On the other hand, I am not an eloquent speaker and, though it may seem childlike, before I open my mouth, I ask the Lord to supply the words. They always seem to come. Thus, I do not have the exact text of what I said that afternoon. But in sum and substance it went like this.

"I want to thank the warden for letting me come here," I said, "and Eugene Logan for extending the invitation in the first place. I don't intend to stand up here and preach at you, I thought we'd have some songs and fun together, but there are a couple of thoughts I'd like to pass on for what they may be worth. You men are locked up and you don't like it much and I don't blame you. But just remember that there are a lot of people outside of these walls who are prisoners just the same, people with locked-up minds and hearts. For some of them the prison gates will never open because they've thrown away the key. For *you* there's hope of release from this prison, but for the man who's put his heart behind bars there's no hope. What I mean to say is that you men are not very lucky to be here, but you could be worse off. I was worse

off, once. Maybe if I told you something about myself . . ."

Then I stopped and laughed and said, "Aw heck, my life
is an open book. You've read all about me and you don't
want to be bored by listening to the story all over again. I
was a drunk, an alcoholic, and I didn't wind up in prison.
But when you're an alcoholic you're shut up in your own
self-imposed prison. And when you try to free yourself
there's no warden to advise you, no parole board to give
you a hand, no executive pardon. You just go on serving
time year after year after year until some miracle gives
you the key to freedom.

"And this release doesn't come as long as there's animosity in you. You've got to get the resentment out of
your system before you can spring yourself from your own
prison. It took me sixteen years to get rid of my animosity,
to break out of stir, so you can see I wasn't very strong.
But now I'm wiser, I hope, and certainly I know how
glorious it is to walk as a free human being, free inside,
with my heart and mind full of love for everyone . . . for
you.

"Gosh, I didn't come to sadden the day, to depress it,
but to make it lighter for us all. There's not a lot I can do,
but I can sing a few songs for you if you'd like that. I've
got some oldies and if you know them I hope you'll sing
along with me. It just occurred to me that it would be nice
if we had something besides Bobby's piano, some rhythm,
maybe. Anybody here play drums?"

[*139*]

There was a shout in a corner of the room and suddenly a blushing young man was being shoved forward. He admitted shyly to playing drums and magically a pair of sticks were produced and a small table placed beside the piano to become his instrument. Bobby Kroll gave an introduction and we went into my songs.

Well, that drummer boy had his own idea about the beat and half the time he wasn't with me, the other half I wasn't with him. He was in a world of his own and often there wasn't room for me. All of which made my ballads sound like some sort of rock 'n' roll. Certainly, a new rhythm was created that day. But it was all great fun and his pals in the audience cheered him on with great pride and loyalty.

As I sang, a change came over the faces before me. My songs do have a brightness to them, and the deep-etched lines of the hardest faces began to soften and twist and gradually assume a smile. Then, at the end of my performance, I went into my regular closing song, "Please tell me when I'll see you again," and walked slowly among the men as I sang the farewell. I saw unashamed tears glistening in their eyes and I got a big lump in my own throat.

Those men weren't crying because I was leaving them, but because the songs I had sung touched something deep inside. If you had asked one of them why he cried, he wouldn't have been able to tell the reason. It was for something intangible—for what has been, what could have been, for what might yet be. The void was there, and in me, too.

I was led back to the warden's office where Eugene Logan was waiting for me. Well, if I had owned a ranch and needed a nice, big, husky ranch hand, Eugene would have been the man for the job. He was six feet two or three and looked something like John Wayne, though a bit heavier and, of course, a good deal younger. He had fair hair and intense eyes. He was nervous, just like the boy next door when he calls on his girl's family and wants to make a good impression. Eugene wanted so desperately to please me, but his shyness kept getting in the way of his efforts. When we turned to the subject of his songs, however, his shyness was drowned in the torrent of his enthusiasm and excitement.

He had sheets and sheets of music to show me, twenty or thirty. "Look," he exclaimed, "look at this one . . . and this one . . . and look here at this one. There just aren't hours enough for me to write about all the beautiful things I see in my mind. The minute my work is done I begin writing songs and sometimes I write all through the night."

I felt like a mother who has to catch her child's hand before he falls and hurts himself. I didn't want to quench his fire, but I didn't want it to consume him, either. I was afraid an obsession might overtake him. "Eugene, please listen to me," I said. "There's only so much you can do. You've got the rest of your life to describe all the beauty you see and feel. So take time with your work."

"I have so much to say, there just doesn't seem time," he cried.

"You'll have time. Go at it slowly and well and sure."

"You know, I sent some to Glenn Miller's brother, who is our minister, and he encouraged me."

"That's wonderful, Eugene."

"Every one of my songs will be dedicated to you," he said.

"No, Eugene, that is not right. If you want to, just one will be enough."

"The one called 'The Search,' I was thinking especially of you when I wrote that."

"Then I'd be honored to have that one dedicated to me."

As we rode back to San Francisco in the dusk, we were all very quiet. I am sure that each one of us came away from this prison with a feeling of gratitude, of having received more than we had given. With all sincerity I felt that God had been good to me in allowing me the privilege of extending my hand in friendship to a lost fellow being and that the warm affection and admiration I received was beyond my worth.

Eugene writes me almost every week. A recent letter of his said, "Many wonderful things have happened to me since you visited here at the prison. To begin with, I have written two numbers that have real meaning. The first is called 'How Shall I See?' and is about a little boy who has lost his sight to cancer. The second is a song called 'Israel' and is about the struggle of a very wonderful people and the plot of good earth they claim as their own. I was visited here by three members of a publishing company who are interested in both songs. I'm going to donate all the money from 'How Shall I See?' to the little blind boy and his family; and the money from 'Israel' will go into Bonds for Israel.

"I received a wonderful letter from Mr. Ben Swig, owner of the Fairmont Hotel in San Francisco. He is very interested in 'Israel' and had it played for Mrs. Golda Meir, the Foreign Minister of Israel. He is also going to send it to New York and have it played for the Israel Ambassador to the UN. What about that?"

Indeed, what about that spirit of Eugene Logan!

It seems to me as though a miracle has taken place that this man, confined for life to a prison cell, has now found a reason to live. I am sure that I myself have really little to do with it. Reading *I'll Cry Tomorrow* may just have been the trigger that set off his emotions to the extent that he became inspired. It was the light of God's gift that showed up in the darkness of Eugene Logan's life.

For whenever we are deeply troubled we have but to look into ourselves to find an answer. We may find that some gift had been lying dormant in us of which we were not aware, a talent that God has given us. And utilizing this latent force we may find the ability to live again with ourselves above the problems that beset us, and learn to give of ourselves to others, which is the greatest gift of all.

7

Searching for the Truth

I have a great and ever present consciousness of God's hand in my life and I wish to make a few observations about religion. Yet, I am beset with misgivings.

Will I offend my people, the Jews, when I say that my conversion to the Catholic Church has taken me too far into Christianity ever to return to Judaism? Will I offend the Christians when I say that I'm inherently so much Jew that I cannot really forget that heritage and honestly think I am the richer because of it? Will I offend the Catholics when I say that despite my love and respect for the Church, I am unable, perhaps because of my own imperfections, to accept completely all man-made laws or dogma?

I don't know. Yet I must say these things. I must be honest about my own confusions. And certainly I must say

[*147*]

that despite those confusions as to church and dogma, I feel close to God. There are many paths that lead to Him, and if mine has been a tortuous and bewildering one, I have never felt deserted by Him.

The above words must clearly indicate that I have no hard and fast answers to give beyond my sure knowledge that God loves us all, Jew and Gentile, Mohammedan and Buddhist, black, yellow, and white.

When my conversion became known to the public, people were quick to write me with both criticism and advice. A young rabbi wrote me: "I studied at Loyola and I too was almost converted to Catholicism, so I know the pull the Church has exerted upon you." Another rabbi wrote a long letter in which he begged, ". . . please tell me what was lacking in Judaism for you . . . where did we fail you?"

A young married woman wrote: "I know I have no right to write you concerning this matter of religion but it might make me feel better to do so. Speaking for all my Jewish friends and for myself, we were always proud that such a one as you stemmed from our race, and with your talent has brought such joy to all peoples. Yet, now we feel abandoned, lost, or shall I say forsaken in your conversion to Catholicism. We assume that because of your trouble with alcoholism you have found solace and peace in a new belief. Judaism has been oppressed since the advent of time and yet has always managed to rear its head because of faith in the Almighty.

"Lillian, we feel you could have found as much consolation in our Psalms and our way of prayer regardless of the fact that your parents did not maintain or strictly adhere to Jewish protocol. However, we wish to conclude with this: namely, we shall not forsake you as you have forsaken us. We shall always await your performances eagerly and wish you and Burt McGuire health and *mazeltov* always."

It disturbed me to have this young woman think I had "forsaken" the Jews, though I was grateful that the tone of her letter was sad, rather than bitter.

Even more difficult for me were the times when people came to me for religious advice and instruction. I had no certain answers for anyone, yet they were demanded of me. One night, after I had finished a show in a midwestern city, I found two young people waiting for me in the club lobby. They must have been eighteen or nineteen, a boy and a girl, holding hands with a desperateness that revealed some deep problem. The boy approached me shyly.

"Miss Roth," he said, "my name is Saul Bernstein. I . . . I read your book and I thought it was very good."

"Thank you, Saul," I said. I waited, knowing he hadn't come just to praise the book.

He turned and beckoned the girl who came up reluctantly, her face flushed. "This is Mary Callahan," he said. "We're engaged."

"How wonderful," I exclaimed. "Congratulations."

"Could we talk to you . . . alone?" the boy asked.

[*149*]

I led them across the street and to my hotel room. The moment the door was shut they both began to talk at once.

"I'm Jewish," he said.

"And I'm Catholic," she said, "and my family doesn't approve of our getting married."

"Nor does my family," he said. "We love each other and we think that's all that matters. Don't you agree?"

She said, "Why should religion come between us? It's not important to us, so why should it be important to our families?"

"Both our families are narrow and prejudiced."

"You'd think we lived back in the Dark Ages, and in Europe, instead of here in America, in the Twentieth Century!"

"Nothing can stop us getting married. Nothing!"

"But we thought if you'd talk to our parents, maybe you could make them understand. Could you talk to them, Miss Roth?"

"But why me?" I protested. "Who am I to give religious advice?"

Saul said, "You've been a Jew and now you're a Catholic. You're wiser than our parents, and they'll listen to you."

I almost had to laugh. "Oh Saul," I said, "wiser than your parents? Did they almost drink themselves into the grave? Did they get married five times? Did they throw away a career, lose all self-respect, lose all their friends, almost lose their minds? Did they do any of these things? Then how can you say that I am the wiser?"

The boy shook his head stubbornly. "I don't care what happened to you in the past. That's what made you wiser, maybe."

"That's what made me compassionate, maybe. But wiser?"

"*You* don't think we should be prevented from getting married because of religious differences, do you?" Mary demanded.

Both of them looked at me and waited for my answer. I had to be very careful to make them understand exactly how I felt about it. I said, "I think you should get married if you can have a good life together. Hurting your parents unduly is not the beginning of a good life."

"But how can we avoid. . . ."

"By trying to understand them, Saul. They're not trying to stop your marriage to Mary out of stubbornness and meanness, but because they honestly think they know what is best for you. They are part of the long and proud tradition of Judaism, and they don't want you to lose it. Remember your Bar Mitzvah? Remember the beauty of the ceremony? The pride in your father's and mother's eyes? And Yom Kippur! Can you honestly say that you went to the synagogue for confessions and prayers without feeling cleansed afterwards? These are the things your parents are afraid you'll lose. You are no less a Jew for marrying a Catholic, I know, but you must make your parents understand you are not turning your back on your inheritance.

"And you, Mary. Your parents have been taught by the priests that your Church is the true Church, the universal Church. For you to slip away from it would, in their minds, endanger your soul. They love you and they try to do what they think is right for you. It's not so much that either your or Saul's parents are prejudiced, it's that they believe what their priests and rabbis have taught them, and they want you to share those beliefs."

"We don't want to defy them and run away to get married," Saul said, "but what are we to do?"

"I think you should separate," I said.

There was a moment of stunned, shocked silence. Both young people looked at me as if I had betrayed them. I had put the advice bluntly so as to impress them . . . and I had certainly done that. The boy opened and closed his mouth several times but no words came. Tears began to gather in the girl's eyes, and I looked away because I didn't want to be diverted from what I thought I had to say.

I repeated slowly, "I think you should separate. That does not mean that you should decide at once to give up each other, but that you should test yourselves. A marriage will be something that will affect the rest of your lives, surely you can pause and make certain."

"You think it's wrong?" the girl asked in a small voice.

"I didn't say that. I'm not the one to judge. Only you and Saul can decide what is right for you two, but I don't think you should rush into that decision. If you two get married it will inevitably mean turning your backs on much of your past, cutting off your roots. It means that you will become different people than you are now . . . different than the ones you each fell in love with. Maybe you will grow together and create something very enduring despite the hurt you give to others, but it is not a step to be taken lightly. Separate for a time, and each of you view this very complicated problem alone, without being influenced by the other. If, after the separation you still ache for each other, are convinced that you cannot find happiness without each other, then that is your sound and considered decision and I don't think anyone should stand between you."

They looked at me in silence and I had a feeling that things would work out for them. I told them I thought they ought to do a lot of praying but that there are certain things God expects us to do ourselves.

"Give your parents a little time. You can't break down a lifetime of inherent beliefs in a day. Be honest, be persistent, be loving. And good luck."

Perhaps my words were of some help; certainly strangers have often helped me in my dilemmas. When a newspaper reporter printed the fact that I was having some difficulty with certain Catholic dogma, I received many letters of advice and some of them were quite profound. I should like to quote one of them. This came from a woman in a small New England town:

". . . I hope you won't resent or be offended by my writing you about religion, but I too am a convert to the Church and I have had my share of difficulties so I think I

can understand how you feel. You probably entered the
Church convinced that you had found the Way and the
Truth and that everything would be smooth sailing from
then on. Only then maybe you ran into some difficulties in
your thinking, things which differed from the Church's
teaching, and you were stumped. You probably feel that
it isn't quite honest to believe so strongly in your own view
of truth and remain within a body of opposing and con-
tradicting ideas.

"I have gone all through this several times since my
baptism. The first year of my conversion I ran into some
atheist college professors who threw me into a tizzy. I
found the very basis of my faith in God being under-
mined. I was not mature enough at the time to realize
that there was a clear solution for every difficulty they
threw my way, if only I had the patience and fortitude to
sit tight and wait for it. But I was determined not to lose
the wonderful gift of my Catholic faith . . . even though
it cost me a terrific struggle, I would force myself to recite
the Profession of Faith which I had made on the day of
my baptism.

"I found comfort at that time in the famous saying of
Cardinal Newman, himself a convert: 'Ten thousand difficulties do not constitute one real doubt.' Gradually the
clouds of doubt cleared away but not without some black
moments. The more I have read and the more I have
studied through the years, the more I am convinced of the
truth of our faith.

SEARCHING FOR THE TRUTH

"But other difficulties have arisen from time to time. Like you, I have often wondered about animals. I have a parakeet who is so smart it is almost uncanny. He seems to know just what he is talking about, and acts almost human at times. I know that there are some dogs who have almost human qualities, too. Although the Church teaches that animals do not have souls, immortal souls, that is, with an after-life, I have read that it is permissible to believe that God has given them a vast amount of natural intelligence. The principle of life that animates them can be called a soul, if you will, but not the same as man's, for they do not possess human reason. I think you would be interested in some of Leon Bloy's ideas on animals. He was the great French Catholic writer of the last century, you know, and somewhere in one of his books he said that he believed the sufferings of innocent animals played their part in the scheme of Redemption. His writings have never been condemned by the Church. We are allowed to have our own theories on a great many things not definitely revealed by God. St. Augustine had some very unorthodox theories on Creation and the fall of Adam and Eve, but he was content to call them merely theories, suspending judgment in favor of the Church.

"There is no way of being absolutely certain about anything, Lillian. The Catholic Church comes closest to providing an answer but there are still some things which we will never be certain about in this life. The Church teaches the things that were revealed by God through our

[155]

Lord Jesus Christ. There are many other secrets which are kept by God behind a locked door. It will only be opened for us when we step through it and enter Heaven. It has to be that way . . . there has to be some mystery about life, for if we were to know all the answers, we would have to be as wise as God Himself! Our finite minds cannot grasp all the mystery that is contained in the universe. If many things were not revealed by God, it must be that they are not really important for us to know.

"The Church uses human logic and reasoning in coming to many of her conclusions outside the realm of revelation. Maybe there is an entirely different explanation for those things, but we will not know in this life. It is hard to do, but I have found that it pays to suspend judgment on difficult things, leaving it to greater minds to seek for the answers.

". . . Your remark in the press about not reaching spiritual perfection made me do a 'double take.' Believe me, it is not an easy state to attain. I daresay some people have spent their entire lives in monasteries and convents and have not even come close to it. Some of the saints have felt that it was still unattainable for them. Perfection will be really 'perfect' only in Heaven, although we can come as close to it on earth as God wills for us and gives us the grace for.

". . . Thanks for taking the time to read this much-longer-than-planned letter. I hope it has been of some benefit to you. I told you at the beginning how I feel really close to you because of your conversion, and I wanted you to know that there were others who have had difficulties and have come through all right without leaving the Church."

What a wonderfully warm letter and, in many ways, what a wise one. That another human being, a complete stranger, should concern herself so deeply with my problem was a very sustaining factor for me. Yet in all honesty, it did not solve that problem, it did not put my mind at rest.

Strange as it may seem, the things that bothered me were little things. For instance, if a baby dies before it has been baptized, the Church says that it does not go to Heaven. Yet I cannot conceive that God, who has allowed the separation of mother and child here on earth, would not reunite them forever in the hereafter. To me, God is all-loving and all-understanding. Though I have never been a mother, I have felt the ache of others who have lost their child. There is not enough time in life to allow them the surcease of forgetting their loss. To most of them their only consolation is that one day, in another world, they will see their baby again. The God I feel I know does not deny, he fulfills.

In going over the words of Christ oh, so many times, I found that He insists that we pray to the Father which is in Heaven. He has never stated that we pray to Christ. Also, I cannot see God as a vengeful God for if he wishes us to love our neighbor and to forgive him, would it not be inconsistent to believe that he would hold the sins of Adam and Eve on a people not yet born?

[157]

There are many things that call my attention and they have troubled me for I know you cannot accept things half-way. God would know the truth.

I was talking to a priest, one day, about my problem, when my little dogs romped into the room. I pointed to them and said, "The Church holds that animals have no soul and cannot go to Heaven. But St. Francis deserted the world and went to live with the animals he loved. Could it be that God would deny St. Francis his animals in Heaven? Does not the Bible say: 'In my father's house there are many mansions?'" The priest smiled and said, "It is strange. I have no answer for you right now."

I have been told that some of these are questions of Faith. Perhaps my faith in man's interpretation of God is weak, but I must suspend decision for myself on these questions. I do not expect to achieve spiritual perfection, but I shall continue to pray for spiritual progress.

Perhaps my Jewishness has complicated my problem. Oh yes, I remain a Jew, regardless of my Christian conversion. I do not believe that being a Jew is merely adhering to a religion that can be put on or off like a cloak. We are a tribe of people with a long history, both tragic and in-spiring, that marks us to this day. And in a way, I was never so aware of my Jewishness as when I became a Christian. It was impressed upon me in a number of ways.

Shortly after my conversion, I went with a friend to a Catholic Ladies Auxiliary meeting, and over tea they be-gan a discussion about Good Friday. Out of this came talk of the problem of the Jew. These people only knew me as Mrs. McGuire and so were unaware that a Jew was among them. In fact, I doubt if these particular women would have thought it possible to be both a Jew and a Catholic. Anyway, they went on and on about the Jews being the killers of Christ.

"Why are the Jews so blind?" one of the women demanded. "Christ is God, yet they deny Him. They refuse to see or understand the miracles."

One woman said, "Perhaps they just don't know the truth."

The first one said, "They don't want to learn the truth."

On and on they went, not realizing they were mouthing the old anti-Semitic propaganda. I kept absolutely quiet until they had finished, then I said, very firmly, "Let me tell you something. Here sits a Jew listening to you. I am a convert to Catholicism, but if I were not, if I had walked in here for the first time to learn, with hope in my heart, to cross over and accept Christ as the Messiah, what do you think would have been my reaction? I would have said, 'Oh, my God, let me out of here!' What you have here is the two-thousand-year-old spiritual iron curtain of prejudice.

"We Catholics follow the Pope, don't we? Well, we don't claim that all the Popes in history were good ones. Some of them at the time of the Spanish Inquisition were pretty bad, but that doesn't alter our faith, or our devotion to the Church. It was much the same with the Jews at the time of Christ. The Jews were divided. When Christ appeared he attracted an immediate following among his own people. All his disciples were Jews, but the majority of the Jews followed their traditional spiritual leaders, the Pharisees. And when these leaders said that Christ was not God's Son but an impostor, they believed them. And, remember, those were days when the belief in evil spirits and devils was strong and so when Christ performed miracles, a lot of people believed him to be doing the devil's work.

"Understand that and you'll understand that you are closer to the Jews than you thought, and the Jews are closer to you than they often admit. You call yourselves Christians. That means you are followers of Christ . . . and He was a Jew! Christianity stems from Judaism. The main thing that separates you and the Orthodox Jews is the Jews' refusal to accept Christ as the Messiah. If and when God wants them all to accept Christ, so it will be."

I imagine I said a lot more to them, and I'm not certain how wise it was for me to speak at all. I was really burned up and couldn't help myself. But this in no way influenced my thinking, because *people* can't destroy faith. And this had nothing to do with the Church itself, for the Church loves everybody, and prejudice is in a minority which cannot prevail. The majority of Catholics I have met are a great, strong, God-loving people.

Father John Roach of Houston once said to me, "I envy your Jewishness because you have the blood of our

Lord and the lineage of our Lady. The Jew is the trunk, Christians the branches."

At another time, when I had been a convert for less than a year, Burt and I went to a church where the priest erred in this respect. He was asking for donations to a building fund and he said, "Please give well. You see how the Jew hates to part with money, yet he gives generously to his temple. You certainly should give as well."

As I heard those words I felt as if I'd been hit. I was outraged and I almost burst out, right there in church. But then I was able to achieve some spiritual balance. I said to myself that this priest represented God, but he didn't think as God did. At this moment he was being only a man, and a very fallible one. I had come here to receive communion and I should take it through his hands, but I didn't have to take what was in his mind. Perhaps this happened to test my faith. I must submerge myself, bury the sin of pride. So I received communion, but I went home very upset.

Burt went to see the priest and said, "We were here for mass this morning and your words shocked my wife. She is a recent convert, a Jew, and your talk upset her deeply."

The priest was mortified and asked Burt to bring me to him. I agreed to go but I was quite nervous. After all, who was I to have set myself against a priest on this question? I felt that I was right, but at the same time I was in awe of a man of the cloth.

He received me very kindly and said, "Dear girl, not for the world would I have hurt you."

"It was not me you hurt, Father, but the Jews."

"I knew the minute the words were out of my mouth that it was wrong." He looked contrite and genuinely sad. But then he added, "How was I to know there was a Jew in church?"

I said, "There was one on the Cross."

I mention these incidents only to make the point that there is human weakness inherent in every great movement, even one so great and good as the Church. But for every incident that upset me, there were a hundred heart-warming ones to compensate. I shall never forget my friendship with the nuns of Watermill, Long Island, who are called "Little Sisters of the Poor." Their humor, love, affection, and humility were a tremendous comfort to me on the death of my mother. And countless other priests, nuns, and brothers I have found full of wisdom and saintliness, always ready to help, always selflessly dedicated to service.

One of the most endearing things about some of the priests I have known is their fine sense of humor. I remember one wonderful man who was hospitalized with a breakdown, yet retained his self-knowing humor. I first heard about him when a priest involved in psychiatric work came to me and asked me to visit this man. He had been a brilliant scholar, but overwork had sent his mind into some sort of relapse.

"But why should *I* visit him?" I asked, really dismayed. "What can I possibly do for him?"

The visiting priest said, "He has often used your book in teaching, citing it as an example of a human being restored to God's grace. He thought very highly of it and we hope that your sudden appearance might give him a new interest in reality, sort of shock him back into the present world."

I agreed to go, but I was petrified. What could I say or do for a man so brilliant and so afflicted? Truly, they judged me beyond my worth, beyond my capacities.

He was in a convent hospital in Canada. When I arrived there, a nun ushered me into his room. I found a handsome, gray-haired man whose face bore the marks of exhaustion. His eyes were vague, withdrawn.

The nun said, "Father, you have a visitor."

He looked at me and seemed uncertain whether I was substance or shadow. I said, "Father, I'm Lillian Roth. A friend of yours asked me to come and visit you and I was very glad to. But now that I'm here, I don't know what to say. Is there anything I can do for you?"

With an effort, he shook his head, "No. But thank you."

I smiled. "Strange, me asking if I can do anything for you. Priests have always done so much for me, given me so much of their wisdom and their strength. You don't need me, you have God. I'm sure you're a lot closer to Him than I am."

[*163*]

A ghost of a smile played over his features. He said, "Not always so. Sometimes He is more interested in His fallen angels who have come back to Him than He is in us." Then, miraculously, a chuckle came from him. He said, "I'm afraid there are times when I bore Him."

My spirit felt lighter when I said goodby to this kindly old man. I had a feeling that he would get well because he had retained a sense of humor about himself.

We sometimes look with awe upon the men of God and it seems to me a mistake because it tends to set them apart from us. Certainly I think these men have a call and a great dedication, but they are also human beings and they share our strengths and our discouragements as well as our humor.

I recently found myself in correspondence with a young American priest, assigned to the back country in Brazil, and though I have never met him, I know that besides being a priest he is a thoroughly delightful human being. The first letter I received from him read:

"Dear Mrs. McGuire: This is just a little note from a Redemptorist Father on the Brazilian missions, to tell you that I was deeply impressed by your biography *I'll Cry Tomorrow*. I had read an article about you in the *Ligourian*, a Redemptorist publication, by Father Arthur Klyber, one of our own men. While in the States on furlough I bought the book and salted it away in my desk for an hour of quiet reading . . . It was a wonderful story of the Grace of God pursuing a soul down through the years . . .

"I imagine you are wondering what kind of a place this is. It is a small town on the frontier of Paraguay, a town something like our western towns, plenty of gun play. This town is deep in the interior and well over a thousand miles from Rio de Janeiro. Our parish is tremendous, it used to be about the size of Italy before it was mercifully divided about two years ago. On the other side of the street is Paraguay, a miserably poor and backward country. The Faith out here, in fact the practice of the Faith in the whole of South America, is very weak. The people have a distorted devotion to images, are steeped in superstition, and about ninety percent of them confine themselves to walking in the Good Friday procession. That about sums up the practice of Faith.

"It is tough work. Life is cheap on the frontier—last week we had three murders, one suicide, and one knifing. That is about par for the course. It would be too long a letter if I delved into life along the mission trails, but if we ever meet I'll tell you all about it. Sincerely yours in Christ, Rev. James Schomber, C.Ss.R."

A few months later he wrote: "Dear Lillian, I hope you do not mind me addressing you as Lillian rather than the more formal Mrs. McGuire. Your kind letter arrived today aboard the usual burro that lugs the mail out to the frontier, and he is no 'Nashua.' I was really delighted with

[*165*]

your letter but felt embarrassed by the enclosed generous gift. I had no intention of putting 'the bite' on you. I am sorely tempted to keep the check as a souvenir, but then I figured you wished to make that sacrifice for the missions. So the gift will paint two classrooms in our parochial school. To me they will be the Lillian Roth rooms. The school was in terrible shape when I arrived here in November—today marks five months that I have been here. I suspect now that the Vice Provincial sent me out here on purpose, knowing that given a job to do I have 'ants in my pants' until it is done. Well, the school roof is fixed up, new ceilings put in, the cracked walls are solid again, a new fence put in, the sisters' convent is almost in good shape. And I got all the necessary funds from friends.

"The little note of lonesomeness you sensed in my letter isn't lonesomeness but a cry of frustration. Jeepers! I have spent eleven years down here in Brazil and at times I get the feeling of working in the dark, the visible results are so meager, yet they all protest to being '*muito catolico*' (very catholic). It piles up on one and at times a plaintive protest escapes, 'Why the waste, Lord?' Then too, when I wrote you, I was at my wits' end trying to trace down all the material I had ordered; it was ordered in November and arrived in March. Then, to get the workers moving—*mama mia!* what a job. They say, '*Amanha, Padre*' (tomorrow, Father). Tomorrow and tomorrow creeps in this petty pace! Shakespeare must have had an inkling of the Latin mentality. It can get one screaming after a while. It is in those moments that a longing sigh goes up for the U.S.A. But then in calmer moments I realize that it is here where obedience has placed me that I can do my best work, say my best prayers and save the souls our Lord wants me to save. But still, that frustration haunts me.

"I have only three more weeks here, for which I say a fervent Thank God. This is tough territory here. Since I arrived we have had fourteen murders in town and the usual quota of knifings and shootings.

"On Tuesday of this week I witnessed a murder. Our Vice Provincial, Father Johnnie Maerz, and myself were in the new church looking over the progress of the construction. At 8:30 A.M. we had gotten to the baptistry and I was explaining to Johnnie the type of window I had ordered made for the baptistry. Naturally we were looking out onto the street. Suddenly, we saw three young men advance on an old man with drawn knives, long, pointed, cruel-looking things. Jeepers! I froze. One fellow sank his knife in the old man's chest, another got him in the back, and the third sank his knife in the old fellow's throat. They kept stabbing him until he fell. The poor old man was trying vainly to shield himself with his arms. Two of the murderers fled, but the third bent down and with the fury of an animal kept plunging his knife into the old man. I bolted out of the church and started to run towards the old fellow to give him absolution. Johnnie was right after me, screaming at me to watch out. But by the time I got to the street the third murderer had fled. Just Father Maerz and myself dared approach the old fellow. Blood was pouring out of him like a geyser. I gave him absolution and Johnnie told me to run for the holy oils. By the time I returned a crowd had gathered. Johnnie turned the old fellow over so I could anoint him. A doctor arrived and declared the old man dead. The body was taken to the hospital. The climax was the police (more feared than the bandits) sent over for our shovel to cover up the blood in the street. The crowd drifted away and life again took up its slow-motion pace."

I came to look forward to the good Father's letters because their humaneness seemed to shed light on my own problems. He didn't lecture me, he didn't advise or direct me, he merely told chattily of his own discouragements and small triumphs. When he cried out, "Why the waste, Lord?", it was a distant echo of my own cries. When he became discouraged over his seeming inability to do his job properly, his mood was common with mine. But he always surmounted his discouragements, he always did his job with good spirit and good humor. His letters and his example were a great tonic for me.

He wrote me that he was being returned to Paranague, a port town in the state of Parana. With touching and forgivable pride he told of a testimonial dinner the priests held for him, and of the words of praise and appreciation they spoke. He was a man both modest and prideful, and I think that's the way we should all be.

From his new post he wrote:

"Paranague is on the coast and life has a few more material embellishments, such as American cigarettes. The
Moore-McCormack ships come in here and keep me rea-
sonably supplied with Camels and Lucky Strikes. This is
an amazing place—our parish covers the waterfront (over
120 miles of it) and dips into the interior for about forty
miles. Communication facilities are primitive. It means
bouncing over horrible dirt roads in Jeeps or cruising the
bays in our boat. The people are just a breath away from
the Stone Age in education. Catholicism is the weak-tea
type, watered down to just a nominal observance of the
Faith . . .

"Say a little prayer that all our sweat, blood, and tears
will someday crack the hard line of total indifference . . .
Happy Christmas and a most encouraging TV and stage
year. Hope that each performance is a stepping stone
to more contentment and to a higher sanctity. Do not lose
any of your champion quality.

"I know that you do have doubts at times, or rather
difficulties in understanding some of the teachings of the
Church, but they will clear up in time . . . Keep close to
our Blessed Mother, say her favorite prayer, the Rosary,
each day and She will take good care of you . . .

"P.S. Some years ago in Tibagi, a small town in the
state of Parana, I had a convert, a Swiss engineer. He had
a tumor on the brain. I explained devotion to Our Lady to
him and told him that in all Redemptorist Churches we

have special devotions to the Mother of God under the title of Perpetual Help. One day during my instruction I offered him a cigarette but he refused it saying, 'Father, I do not smoke on Wednesdays any more. It is the only pleasure I have left in life and the only thing I can offer the Mother of God.' I told him that I was sure that Our Lady would grant him great grace. He answered, 'Father, she has already given me that grace—it came to me in the guise of this illness. When I was healthy I never did give a thought to my soul. God allowed me to suffer and then sent you to instruct me and make me think about my soul's salvation. I do not ask for anything else.' What a guy!"

Yes, and what a man is Father James Schomber!

I have many wonderful memories of such men and women of the Church and it saddens me to think how upset they will be when they learn of my indecisions. For their sakes I almost want to say, "Yes, I believe all the dogma and don't you worry for my soul." But, of course, I cannot. I must continue to seek truth in my own way.

Where exactly do I stand? Inside the Church or out? I honestly don't know. I withhold myself from certain man-ordained laws, but I'm not at all certain that this means I am no longer a member of God's universal Church. Maybe He still considers me a member in good standing. Or, maybe He knows that all my life I have had to depend on someone or something and maybe He wants me to walk alone for a little while and see how I fare.

I am comforted by the words recently spoken to me by Father Gallery in Chicago. He said, "Lillian, what you are going through is not your fault, not my fault, not the Church's fault. It has to do with God's plan for you. He will clarify things for you in His time."

8

It's a Wonderful World

"An entertainer is only as good as his audience." That is an old adage in show-business. The show is completely successful only when audience and performer become one, when they share a deep, warm vibration that sweeps them along, making them happily expectant. This exhilaration cannot be created by either of them alone—they accomplish it together, or not at all.

Walt Whitman must have had this in mind when he said, "To have great poets, there must be great audiences, too."

I know, for instance, that you can never put any audience into a neat category ahead of time and then relax, expecting to establish that wonderful vibration automatically. Each time you go on the floor you must feel your way, probe, test, and experiment until you hit just the right tone and mood to unlock their hearts.

There are a few generalities you can count on, however. A hotel audience is generally better behaved than a night-club audience. Let me give as example two places I've worked—the *Chez Paree* in Chicago, and the "Persian Room" at New York's Plaza Hotel, each tops in its field. At the *Chez Paree* the audience is usually composed of out-of-towners who have come to the Loop for business or pleasure and this is their big night for howling. They want to whoop it up, and you'd better be going their way, fast and full of fun, or they'll leave you "alone in a crowd."

The "Persian Room," on the other hand, is more apt to be full of people who are sophisticated and accustomed to night life and therefore less boisterous. At the "Persian Room" there is no chorus line, no comedian, no other acts to precede you, and you must create the mood. In a hotel your contract usually requires that there be no service of food and liquor during your act, which cuts down on the noise and distractions and focuses the entire attention upon your performance. One reason for this is that no performer can compete with a steak on a sizzling plate. And silver has its own music that can drown out any orchestra.

But even in the "Persian Room" there will be different kinds of audiences at different hours of the night and on different days of the week. At the dinner show (nine o'clock) you'll find a quieter audience than at the midnight show. They will just have had their dinner and they don't feel like jumping around and shouting hooray. You can't come at them with a slap-bang night-club routine because it will be a shock to them. You must begin more gently, increasing your intensity only after you've been on for ten or fifteen minutes.

The people at the supper show, on the other hand, have already been out on the town for the evening, usually at the theater, and they're gay, vibrant, and eager for more excitement. So you work this show a little brighter and faster. As a rule, the songs are the same, but the tempo, the spirit is different. The audience creates the mood, and you set the pace.

There is no show on Sunday, and then tired old Monday arrives, and I mean tired. Everybody seems a little beat, the orchestra, the waiters, the customers and even Lilly, too. "Monday's child is full of woe because the people got no go." However, with such an audience you can sometimes establish a camaraderie, and you can throw in ad libs and sort of take them into the act. If you can get them moving, they have a lot of fun.

The mid-week audiences are the most sophisticated; they are people who don't plan their entertainment but are apt to decide on the spur of the moment to go to the Plaza for dinner and catch the show. Friday night is generally a family audience; parents bringing their children to see the show because they can sleep late the next day.

Saturday night is the most difficult audience, for these are the planners, the people who have carefully read all the ads and weighed the advantages of the various shows being offered. It is often a mixed audience, part middle-aged people and part youngsters, but both of them definitely want their money's worth. If you can win this audience, convince them they didn't make a mistake when they chose you over all the other attractions in the city, then they're just great.

Sometimes you'll get an audience that's split into two different racial or sociological groups and this creates a special problem for the performer. I remember one evening at the "Persian Room" when I came on stage and knew at once that something was constrained about the audience. During my first number I studied them and discovered that about half were leading socialites from New York's "400," and the other half was made up of Jews who were being very polite, but extremely reserved and dignified. They weren't enjoying themselves because they were afraid that if they were the least bit extroverted they would offend someone.

How often have we Jews been accused of loud aggressiveness? The truth is that there are many people who can match us in that department. Take a lusty Irishman, now. When he ties one on, God bless him, the leprechauns way over in Ireland can hear him.

But there was the problem, half of my audience too self-conscious to let its pleasure surface. I couldn't very well stop and lecture them right in the middle of my act, I was hired to sing. I gave Bobby Kroll a cue and we went into, "It's a Big, Wide, Wonderful World We Live

[178]

In." I was telling them, in song, that this was a wonderful world and that this was a wonderful evening, not only for a few but for everyone. I sang directly to them, and they knew it. When I finished, they laughed and applauded in a fine, relaxed manner, and from then on we were all one and had a wonderful time.

One thing I always watch for is a hostile table. Such a table can infect the entire room unless it is won over. At such times I play directly to that table until I know I have it with me. I remember one time I came out on the floor for the dinner show at the Fairmont Hotel in San Francisco and was received warmly by the entire room except for one table occupied by a man and his wife. The woman kept her back half-turned toward me and glared at me over her shoulder. I hadn't finished my first song before I had it figured. She resented me.

She was about my age, but she had let herself go a bit. She hadn't fixed her hair too carefully, she'd put on weight, and now she just felt unglamorous and uncomfortable. And here was I all gussied up; I was helped by lighting and make-up, and my dress designer was no slouch when it came to making the figure look svelt. I was acting light and gay, as if I didn't have a care in the world, and her husband was looking at me as if he was back in his college days.

She was thinking to herself, "Why did I ever let Joe come here? Now he's comparing me with her and wishing I looked that way."

Without drawing attention to the fact, I began to play directly to that woman. I wanted her to relax and have a good time. I wanted her to be happy with Joe, and Joe with her. The next song was a long arrangement and I'm always a bit winded when I finish it. But this time I puffed more than necessary and then I grinned rather sheepishly and said to her, "Gee, I can't understand this. I never puffed when I sang this song in 1929."

I could see a smile in her eyes as she turned around to her husband. Now she relaxed. She was mine. When it came time for me to invite members of the audience to dance with me, she nudged her husband and urged him to volunteer, which he did. She applauded loudly and happily when we finished a brisk foxtrot around the floor. Making her evening a success made my evening a success.

My dance routine comes in about the middle of the show, after the audience has had time to warm up. I choose about six different men from the audience to dance with and until they get on the floor they don't know whether the orchestra is going to do a rumba or a waltz, a Cha-cha or a rock-'n'-roll number.

It's a lot of fun and joy when you can get your patrons up to dance, but I think we really reach the top of enjoyment when we can get a very dignified or prominent man up to dance. Of course, there are many reasons why some people don't dance; they may be shy or their heart might not allow them to dance; they may have an affliction like my husband, and I never insist on anyone getting up. But as a rule, if one starts to dance they all go. Dignified or prominent men, although they look formal and formidable, are usually very good sports. I remember I was quite excited when Adlai Stevenson came to hear me. I had always liked his way of speaking and as I passed his table I was just wondering, should I ask him? Then I decided, yes, I will! I went over and suggested he get up and dance with me and he jumped up immediately and turned to the charming young lady with him, just like a little boy asking permission. Was it all right? It all happened in a split second, her lashes just butterflied in acquiescence.

I expected Mr. Stevenson to tower over my five-feet-six-inches—but there was nothing above me. I looked ahead and straight into his eyes. That did it. I tripped like an awkward school girl and landed on his foot. He was very gallant and said, "Oh, I am sorry— My fault."

I said, "It was very kind of you to get up because it pleases people when a man of your stature proves to be a good sport."

He smiled quite a wonderful smile and replied gently, "It was kind of you to ask me."

Celebrities in general are not too pleased when called on publicly. They too want a certain privacy and the right to sit unnoticed and enjoy the show. But getting up to dance with me never seemed to annoy them.

I've danced with Liberace. He does the darnedest, cutest Charleston. At the *Sahara*, Ray Bolger got up with me. I hadn't seen Ray in about twenty-five years and when

I asked him he got up and did the rock 'n' roll, and, of course, the audience just adored it. Bob Hope came in the next night and got up and danced with me. Bing Crosby was at the dinner show and I hadn't seen Bing for a good many years. He sat right down in the center, and I was in a very strange position. I know Bing usually sits in the background and tries to be inconspicuous, but this time he sat in the center and I imagined he didn't mind being seen. But he wasn't wearing his toupee, and I didn't know whether to ask him to dance because I didn't want to embarrass him. And yet, I wondered why he sat in the front if he didn't expect me to ask him. So, Bing, I don't know whether I owe you an apology; and if I owe you a dance I hope you'll ask me one day. Actually, I don't think Bing was going my way that particular night. But then he had a very lovely lady to look at; I could hardly expect it.

I danced with Kirk Douglas, and I can remember his dancing because he has a dimple in his chin, and it was over my head and it just intrigued me. I was looking for the devil within. And I danced with Tyrone Power. When I first went into pictures, Tyrone Power was one of my favorites. I remember that when I was invited to parties, if Tyrone was there—well! There was always something, some quality and charm about him, that set him apart from the rest. He's what a picture actor should be like, handsome, manly without appearing to be the matinee idol. I remember I was working in Detroit when he came to my show. He was doing a show with Katherine Cornell and he had on a beard that brushed my forehead when we danced. Let me tell you, girls, it was fine!

One evening I invited Mr. Morgan, the banker, to dance with me and he accepted. He's an elderly, handsome, and rather stern-looking man. I cued Bobby to give us an easy waltz, but Mr. Morgan had his own ideas. He went into a German waltz with its great hops and whirls, and the audience had a fine laugh watching me trying to keep up with him. He had a keen sense of enjoyment and was glad that everyone was having a good time. He realized they were not laughing *at* him, but that we were all laughing together.

I've had priests come to my shows without their collars so as not to make other people uncomfortable, and not knowing they were priests I invited them up to dance with me. They were always good sports about it and kept their true identities secret until after the show. One time I got a partner onto the floor for a waltz and in the middle of it switched to a rumba. "I'm a rabbi," he whispered to me, so we quickly went back to the waltz.

The more exhausted I get from the dances the more fun the audience has. I usually invite a teen-ager for the last dance and we do a jitterbug. By the end of that I'm really winded and the audience is delighted. They think it's youth that has done me in, forgetting that by the time I get to this boy I've already done a half dozen dances. Or is time really marching on?

There are regional differences in audiences, of course.

The people in the large eastern cities demand a more subtle entertainment, while in the Middle West they are pleased with a simple and direct style. In the South they like a natural bombastic delivery.

As for prejudice in the South, I know it has been felt by a few performers, but happily not by me. Where it has happened it's been due, I'm certain, to a handful of agitators who can whip up evil and upset the majority who really have no malice in their hearts.

I pray that some day, in the not too distant future, the same fair play and affection will be given socially to our fellows that is now given professionally.

To me, Negroes are the greatest entertainers we have. There may be some white people in the profession with better voices or more polished interpretations, but none can approach the natural, bone-deep rhythm of the top Negro entertainers. When I'm not working I make every effort to see and hear such great stars as Nat Cole, Lena Horne, Pearl Bailey, and Louis Armstrong. Even the lesser names can often teach me things that my lifetime in show-business has not.

When I was about nine and doing a vaudeville act with my sister Ann, who was seven, we were often booked into the same show with the late Bill Robinson. Between shows, because he liked us, he'd teach us tap steps. He showed us how not to look as if the dance was killing you, how to do the steps with such ease that you can hear a tap with your feet hardly seeming to leave the floor.

In one or two of my songs I try to emulate the artistry of these performers. In "You Can't Take It With You," I use some of the dialogue I heard when I experienced the excitement of a revival meeting down South. An old, white-haired Negro preacher, with a smile that lit up his face, welcomed his flock gently at first, but then storm clouds darkened his brow and he thundered his warning that you can't go to Heaven on the installment plan, and that you "can't take it with you" when you go. He warned they were behind on their debt to the living, and they'd better put something in the collection box, stop hoarding their money and start doing right.

Wherever I sang that song in the South people loved it. The Negro maids and waiters would stand in back of the club and, along with the white patrons, clap hands to the beat and shout for the Kingdom to come. At those times no one was aware of color, we all were in another world. In a world as it should be.

The same excitement was derived from the song "Sing You Sinners," which I introduced in the motion picture *Honey*, back in 1930. I use a modern beat, but with overtones of a Negro spiritual, and the song has a universal feeling that never fails to stir the audiences and make them feel as one.

I had a Negro maid who traveled with me for a time and one day, while we were talking about the school situation and other aspects of de-segregation, she said, "Sure, I want my child to go with white children and to attend white schools because I want him to know white people so he can learn how to live with them. I don't want him to grow up fearing and hating them, the way I was taught to do. But I don't want my boy to marry a white, I want him to marry his own kind. That's the only way to happiness."

In her way she was saying that we are all part of God's family. George Washington Carver expressed the same feeling when he said: "We are united as the palm of our hand and separate as the fingers on it." Certainly the whole hand suffers when any finger is wounded.

To have fun in a club or anywhere else, we must all like each other. But sometimes we have to battle out complex problems before we can dance together and sing together. But we can do it, we can accomplish it, because basically we all want to.

In talking of the many different aspects of the entertainment field—the clubs, the audiences—I should also not overlook the younger people, our teenagers, who comprise a great part of my following.

So much has been said about teen-agers, so much head-shaking and lip-pursing, that I'd like to have my little say here: I think the majority of our teen-agers are pretty wonderful. I'm going to go further, really out on a limb, and say that I think the Lindy Hop, the Shuffle, the Jitterbug and Rock 'n' Roll are all pretty cool. When I think back to the days when *we* were teen-agers and doing the Westchester, the Black Bottom, and the Charleston, I can't honestly say that Rock 'n' Roll is any more earthy than our dances were. The beat has changed over the years, but the teen-agers haven't, and if we oldsters (beg your pardon—we mature people) don't like what we see in our youngsters, then we wouldn't have liked ourselves thirty years ago.

No, as a rule it is seldom the teen-ager who is inattentive or noisy or brash in the night clubs; they're much too interested in entertainment for that. Often they are in love, and that is a very serious business. It pleases me when I see a group of teen-agers in the audience, because the part of my act that is nostalgic gives them a kick—for them it is new and different.

Two years ago I played the fashionable Fairmont in San Francisco and the very next week jumped to Chubby's in Camden, New Jersey. Chubby's catered mostly to teen-agers before it was destroyed by fire recently, and most of its bookings consisted of recording stars and a lot of rock-'n'-roll combos. Well, those kids were as attentive and respectful during my act as the audience had been at the Fairmont, and their applause just as generous if not more so. When I finished my show and started walking and singing through the room I heard one young girl say to her boy friend, "What a crazy act! But man, she's cool!" That was one of the nicest compliments I ever received.

No discussion of audiences would be complete without mention of my old compatriots, the drunk and the alcoholic. And the two are quite different, of course. The alcoholic is nervously but quietly drawn into himself and causes no trouble, whereas the occasional drunk is the noisy one and can really disrupt your act if he has a mind to, and he usually does.

There are exceptions to this, of course. I recently had to cope with an alcoholic who was pretty difficult to handle. When I first came on the floor my senses flashed a signal. I spotted this man seated to my right and slightly behind me at a ringside table. His quiet face—youthfully aged—brought back to me so sharply my own battle with the bottle that my heart went out to him. He received my first smile and bow. I guess that was a mistake. It seemed to rouse him, bring him out of himself. And I became his target.

I have a special song about a boy I loved and lost by the name of John. This seemed to amuse our friend, the alcoholic, and when I went on to other material he kept repeating, "Dear John." Whenever there was the slightest pause he would fill it with his quiet voice repeating, "Dear John." No matter what I sang or said, he'd answer, "Dear John."

Then I came to my monologue where I observe that the majority of modern songs are written to glorify women, and I give examples of "A Pretty Girl Is Like a Melody," "She's Lovely to Look At." I go on to say that every time a song is about a man there doesn't seem to be anything nice to be said: "He's Mean to Me," "Just a Gigolo," "It cost me a lot, but there's one thing that I've got—My Man," "Jim Doesn't Ever Send Me Pretty Flowers," "Along Came Bill, an ordinary guy." Well, after I cite these examples I say to the men in the audience that I'm sure we girls don't really feel that way about them, we think they're pretty wonderful.

This night, however, our alcoholic friend felt a song coming on. I sang, "Along Came Bill . . ."

He sang, "Just an ordinary John."

I came to "Jim . . ."

And he cut in with, "John Doesn't Send Me Pretty Flowers."

He was ruining my timing and, of course, ruining whatever humor there was in the routine. Finally I stopped dead and said to the audience, "You know this man reminds me of the person who's seen a murder mystery and now he's telling you the whole plot before you can see it. And you know something else? In a few minutes there's going to be a murder right here in this room."

Everybody laughed, including my woozy aide, and during the rest of the show he was all for me. As always, for my final number I walked among the tables and sang "Please Tell Me When I'll See You Again," and I made a point of going to his table to touch his shoulder. He whispered, "I'm sorry," and I answered, "I understand."

Now, the drunk, the noisy part-time drinker, can be more difficult. He wants to join show business, be a part of the act, and generally the best way to handle him is to invite him to come right up on the floor. In most cases this will quiet him down, because deep inside he knows he's behaving like a bully and he prefers not to have the spotlight on him during the process. If he does come up, then you let him join you in a song or a dance and he'll soon discover that he's not quite so talented as he thought, for his dancing legs have turned to some rubbery substance and those toes that twinkled so gaily earlier in the evening are now suddenly magnetized to the floor. His once well-pressed suit has taken the spot test and failed. His voice, once so penetrating from a ringside table, has now left him. Here is pathos, the wind-battered scarecrow with the mouth agape but soundless. He is happy to escape the spotlight and be quiet for the rest of the evening.

One night, in the *Chez Paree* in Chicago, there was a drunk who kept his back turned toward me and continued to talk to his table in a loud voice while I tried to perform. He was talking as if he knew me personally and was familiar with all the intimate details of my life—how old I was, how I used to drink, the fact that one of my husbands had beaten me up, that I had been in a mental institution. He reported all this in a brutal and boastful tone.

I let him continue until the audience throughout the room knew what he was up to, then I said to him, "I can hear you all right. Can you hear me?"

He said, "Yeah, too well."

"Well, you're fortunate because you can leave, but I can't. I'm being paid to do a job here, and the audience has paid to see me do it. So you can see, one of us has got to go." Then I sang, "For all we know we may never meet again. Before you go, make this moment sweet again." It subdued him. He applauded, and went on applauding to the end of my act—at the right times, of course.

No matter what the provocation, I don't believe in making a big fuss, or calling the waiters, or stamping off the stage. The majority of people come wanting to see a show and have a good time and I try to give them that, ignoring the small minority who cause unrest. And the audience is usually with you when you have trouble with a heckler. You're surrounded by unknown friends who are all for fair play, so it is unreasonable to spoil their pleasure by giving rudeness the dignity of retaliation.

I must confess, however, that I'm not always in complete control of my emotions. There are times when your physical and emotional stamina are worn down so far you lose control. There was one such day in New York a while ago when I got up at ten o'clock in the morning (I had been up until five the night before) in order to do a recording. I rehearsed all afternoon, then attended a benefit dinner, where I sang. I did my nine-o'clock show and gave three interviews, which I always feel are a privilege, for without the press we remain unknown. Then a young rabbi came to see me at about eleven o'clock, by appointment, wishing earnestly to know where Judaism had failed me, or I had failed it, and why I had joined the Catholic Church. I told him that I didn't believe any religion failed a person if he truly held it. I revealed to him that though I had joined the Catholic Church I was having difficulty in accepting some of the dogma. I looked to the priests and the rabbis to give me the answers, certainly I couldn't get them on my own. But maybe God would reveal things to me in His proper time. We talked for quite a time and such a discussion would be exhausting in itself without all the other events of the day.

When the time arrived for my supper show at one o'clock in the morning, I could hardly keep my eyes open. I was beat. Sure enough, that night there was a leftover heckler from New Year's Eve sitting at ringside. I just didn't have any reserve of strength to handle him properly. I turned on him and said in a cutting tone, "I know you're clever but why don't you sit further back and be clever? How about behind the entrance to the exit, so you can give the man in the street a break?"

The audience laughed, but uneasily because it was clear to them that I was angry. And though I worked doubly hard the rest of that show, I had lost contact with the audience and was never quite able to reestablish the mood of easy, relaxed fun.

Usually, when I'm let down or discouraged I'll say a little prayer before my show. It's not that I expect God to cater to me, but I pray for contact with Him, and for the ability to tap the extra energy I need. Then, miraculously, as I think in a positive way, the fatigue does disappear and I'm replenished.

Sometimes, I'll think of my mother, and I'll say to her in my mind, "This one is for you, Katie, just for you." Or it will be for my dad, who was always convinced that "you can't kill talent." Then I'll go out on that floor and give everything I've got, knowing how pleased with me they would be if they were sitting in the audience.

I add new songs and material to my routine as I go along. I like to keep the act fresh, but I never use risqué or "blue" material. That's why I am able to perform for all groups, including teen-agers and religious people. Not only do I not want to offend them, but I am personally uncomfortable with such material.

One song I was never too happy with was "Eadie Was a Lady." Ethel Merman had sung it on stage, and I had done it in the movies. It was considered something of a standard, and not particularly offensive to anybody. Yet there was one line in it that I considered vulgar and I was always embarrassed when I sang it. Still, I kept the song in because people asked for it so often.

One evening in Boston a priest came to see my show and I knew he was in the audience. He was a broad-minded man, a chaplain in a veterans hospital outside of town, and I knew he had come to ask me to entertain the patients. When I came to that dubious line, it stuck in my throat. I choked.

After the show, the priest and I had a pleasant talk and made arrangements for my appearance at the hospital. He was about to leave when I said, "Father, was there anything in my act that bothers you?"

He smiled. "Is there anything in the act that bothers *you?*"

"Yes," I said, "there is."

"Well, if it bothers you, take it out, for yourself, not for me."

I don't sing that song any more, even on request.

Time changes audiences too. They are different today from what they were when I first started in the business back in the Roaring Twenties. Gone is the frantic drunkenness, the hysterical race from one night spot to another, the never-ending search for new thrills. Today the audiences are much quieter. I don't mean that they lack warmth, for they are generous in their response to a greater degree than ever before. But there is a dignity, almost a serenity about them, that was missing in previous years.

Strangely, I think this is because of the unsettled state of the world. People know that if everyone isn't calm a war could start tomorrow, and war means a bomb on their city, their home, their loved ones. They have faced this ugly reality and learned to live with it. It's almost as if they have made peace with God, and have looked at the worst there is and found it supportable.

And so they dine quietly with their families, and they go home earlier. There is more love in their hearts because suddenly everything is so very precious.

9

Victory and Defeat

Success is not pleasure gained, it is victory over defeat. It is the will to win when the odds are against us. And the greatest victory is over ourselves, over our own weaknesses and fears.

There is no victory in climbing to the top by pushing another down and using him as a stepping stone. The fruits of success are plentiful and available to all of us. We don't have to take what another man has earned.

God, the Planner, has given each of us a particular plot to develop and He expects us to do it fully, not just half-way. If He dropped me into the entertainment world, then He expected me to make the most of the opportunities there, to try to the full extent of my abilities.

A young fan of mine, thirteen-year-old Lynn Raymond, recently asked my advice on how to become a movie star.

I smiled a little to myself when I read her letter because she had actually answered her own question by enclosing this bit of verse:

"Sitting still and wishing
Makes no person great;
The good Lord sent the fishing
But you must dig the bait."

The "bait" you dig in show business is of an amazing variety. First, of course, there are the long hours and years of study to acquire the necessary skills, and you never stop trying to perfect them. Later, if you've become well established in the business, perhaps even a star, there is the constant fight to climb on upward, or at least not to slip back. It becomes necessary to spend considerable time and thought on publicity and promotion and billing. A star is a star as long as people think he is, and you have to keep them aware of you.

I have long passed the stage where I get a personal thrill, an ego lift, out of seeing my name up in lights. But I know that if I'm to continue in the business I love, I'd darned well better work to keep it up there. All this is to explain about a fight I had a couple of years ago.

At the time, MGM was filming my book. The studio was spending a lot of money on publicity, running full page ads which carried a large picture of me and called the picture "The Lillian Roth Story." About this time I was booked into one of the largest hotels in the West. I'm not going to mention the name of the hotel or the real name of the owner, though he is notorious for treating his performers and employees badly. I'll call him Harry Burns.

Two weeks before I was to open in his club, there came a long distance telephone call from Harry Burns. Burt took the call, listened for a time and then said, "I don't know, Harry. Lillian wouldn't *have* to do it, you know. The contract calls for sole headline billing. But wait a minute and I'll discuss it with her." He put his hand over the mouthpiece and turned to me. "Harry wants you to share booking with another star and take equal billing."

"Why?"

"A new hotel is opening up during our run and it's booked some big names. He's worried about the competition and wants to strengthen the show."

"What do you think, Burt?"

"You've fought a long, hard battle to win top place, honey. I hate to just give it away. It's okay in the night clubs, they've got to have a multiple act bill, but not in hotels."

"But if he's in trouble . . ."

"You'll outdraw anyone. I know you will!"

"Who does he want to book with me?"

"A comedian." He mentioned the name of a top-flight entertainer.

"Oh, for gosh sakes, Burt! Let's not be difficult. Go on, tell Harry I'll share my billing equally with the comedian and be glad to."

Two weeks later we arrived to find the marquee of the hotel carrying the comedian's name in big lights and below it, in letters less than half the size, "Lillian Roth."

The posters flanking the door had my name below the other star's in small print. I knew that the entertainer himself had nothing to do with this. It was Harry Burns breaking his word. I felt that this handling of my billing would hurt me because a lot of important people were arriving for the opening. They would read the papers and see the billing and then my position would be lowered in the whole entertainment world. I didn't want this to happen.

I looked for Mr. Burns but couldn't find him before the show. Perhaps it was just as well. It was a good show and I didn't want to upset everything with an argument. I'd catch him later.

Finally, the next afternoon, I found the king of this domain in his office. "Mr. Burns," I said, "my billing is wrong and not at all according to our mutual understanding."

"Oh, really?" he said.

"I agreed to share equal billing. It is not equal—I don't even get fifty percent of the billing."

"Well, there's been some mistake, Lillian. I'll take care of it tomorrow."

I left his office thinking that maybe it *was* an oversight and that probably his reputation for knocking people down was exaggerated, for he had certainly been courteous to me.

The next day there was no change; the billing remained the same. On the fourth day, I sent a note to Mr.
Burns which read: "I do so admire a man who can be
trusted, who has a word of honor. My name is still not in
the advertisements—the billing hasn't been changed." To
me it seemed a mild enough statement considering the
situation. Shortly after noon, while walking through the
lobby of the hotel, a great roar emanated from the barbershop. There sat Mr. Burns, my letter gripped in his
hand, his face contorted in rage.

"You!" he shouted. "Come in here!"

Everybody in the vicinity turned as I started slowly toward him.

"How dare you," he stormed, "how dare you write such
a letter?"

"Mr. Burns, how dare you violate your agreement?"

"Keep quiet! No one has ever dared to question my
word before."

I held the morning newspaper up. "Look, do you see
my name in the ad?"

He slapped the paper out of my hand. His face had
gone into deep purple. He pointed at a chair and thundered, "Sit down!"

Now, fierce tempers tend to frighten me, not because I
am afraid of them but because I am afraid of my own lack
of control when I have been put in an unfair position. I
know that in the past my losing control has done much to
hurt me.

As I stood before Mr. Burns I could feel pressure building within me. I held myself still, rigid. I felt a cold sweat coming over me as the people in the barbershop stared and the crowd outside gaped in at me. When I spoke my voice was shaking. "Don't you order me around, Mr. Burns. You may be the god of this establishment and scare the people who need their jobs, but you're not my God. My God's above me. I've met your kind before, men who turn mean with too much power."

"I'll fix you!" he cried. "I'll give you only twelve minutes on the show. Use one more minute, and I'll have you blacked out."

I rushed out of the shop. I wanted so hard to cry. I wanted to hide my tears. I ran blindly, and in my mind I was running toward the apron strings of the lovely woman who was not with me any more. For at moments like this I am a child again, and I ache for my mother's arms.

When I collected myself a bit, I realized that the behavior of Burns was not only a blow to my sensitivity as a person and my pride as a performer, his order also created a serious problem. My act ran at least thirty to thirty-five minutes, with all the special arrangements, and to cut it to twelve would just about destroy it. I don't usually like to stay on the stage too long, but it does take time and thought to get the feel of an audience.

I went to my room and tried to think things out. I looked in the mirror and I talked to myself. Couldn't I have handled this situation a little bit better? Couldn't

I have checked myself? Then I thought: no, this man didn't understand quietude. If his word meant nothing, what good would talk have done? And I realized once again that God does not want us to be subservient to any man.

I put in a call for the local representative of my union. He was out of the office and I left a message for him. When it was time for the dinner show, I still had not heard from him. Backstage I found a note waiting for me: "The management reminds you that you are to do not more than twelve minutes." I spoke to the orchestra leader.

"Good Lord, Lillian," he exclaimed, "how can you cut your act to twelve minutes? It will mess up all your arrangements."

"I know it, but I couldn't get the union representative today. For this show we'll just do a few of the quick oldies, 'Goody, Goody' and 'Ain't She Sweet?'"

We started to sort out the music when the stage manager came up to me and said, "I'm supposed to black you out after twelve minutes."

"Larry, don't do that," I begged. "I'm doing my best to cut my act, but I can't time applause and I might run thirty seconds over."

"I can't take orders from you," he said abruptly, "I'm working for Mr. Burns. At the end of twelve minutes you're black."

Was this what I had worked for all these past years?

Here was the stage manager, a man I considered my friend, and I was bewildered by his attitude. Later, after it was all over, I was able to understand that this man hadn't really turned against me, he was just afraid of Mr. Burns. His blustering was to cover up that fear. I really felt sorry for him.

I got through the show although the audience was a little bit puzzled at my rushing off stage so quickly. Many of them questioned me about it later.

The next day I got hold of the union representative and explained how Mr. Burns was violating my contract. "Well," he said, "it will take time. Just be patient."

"I've been patient for almost a week," I replied.

Things never did straighten out. I later discovered that the union official was working for Mr. Burns on the side, handling his chorus line. The union eventually found out about it and replaced the man, but not soon enough to help me. I could have walked off, but I still was in a position where people had their eyes on me, were measuring me, not only as a performer but also as a person. There still were many people who, even after all these years, wondered if I would revert to alcohol. They were surprised that my sobriety had extended over the period it has, they didn't realize it had become part of my life to be a sober person. They thought that it was a day-to-day wonder and accomplishment.

My performances were not too happy for the rest of the engagement. And even the other artists on the program got irked by the treatment I was receiving. The dancer on the bill went to Burns. "You're ruining the show," he said. "I really don't care how much you cut me, but these people are coming in to see Lillian." Burns told him to mind his own business.

When the producer of the show, a dear friend of mine, heard what was happening, he flew in from Hollywood. He told Burns, "This is ridiculous to ruin the show just because you're sore at Lillian. Take some advice from me."

But Mr. Burns took advice from nobody.

I must confess that I was very upset not to be able to give the public what I felt they wanted to hear and see. I said to Burt, "I don't think I can go on. What happens if I leave?"

"If you mean will you get paid, the answer is yes. And if Mr. Burns takes it to arbitration, he'll lose. But . . ." Burt let the "but" hang in the air. I knew what he had left unsaid. I knew before I had asked the question that I couldn't walk out. I had to take it.

Miraculously, my life off stage became a very pleasant one. I was sustained by the affection and admiration of all the employees of that hotel. I noticed it first when the bellboys and waiters began to give me those extra courtesies that cannot be bought. Everybody greeted me with a special warmth, with "good mornings," and "good evenings," and "How is it going, Lillian?"

The spirit and atmosphere of the place was wonderful —off stage. It seemed as if all the employees had appointed themselves my spiritual bodyguards, cheering for me because I was able to face up to the man who held them subjugated.

During the last week of the engagement, whenever I walked into the dining room, I noticed that waiters would be whispering together, turning their eyes in my direction like little boys with a big secret. I couldn't imagine what was going on. But I soon found out. The night my show closed, one of them, as spokesman, pulled me aside and handed me a mother-of-pearl overnight bag and a velvet box. Inside the box was a gold charm in the shape of a miniature airport. On it was engraved, "Bon voyage to a good sport."

When I left the hotel, I still had only second billing. No doubt, Mr. Burns felt that he had had his victory. But in truth he had failed. He was surrounded by fear and animosity, and I had been surrounded by affection. The Harry Burnses of this world never win anything of value.

10

A Shadow Vanishes

One night, when I was playing a hotel in Texas, a hand-some young Army major presented himself backstage and asked if I could find time to come to a nearby veterans' hospital and sing for the men. I said that of course I'd come.

Until you've played before a hospital ward you don't know what a warm and responsive audience really is. And it makes you feel good inside to have been able to help just a little. I said something to this effect to the major.

He shook his head, "We had something else in mind this time, Miss Roth. This particular audience probably won't respond at all."

"Why is that?" I asked.

"You see, we want you to sing to our 'lost men.' "

"Lost men? What do you mean?"

"Our mental cases, the psychotics. We have a ward of about sixty men who have lost all contact with reality, most of them schizophrenics. Not one of them will speak, or give any indication of hearing when spoken to. These are vets from both World Wars, and from the Korean War. They are living shut up in their own private, tortured worlds. We've never tried to give them a show, or any sort of entertainment, because we were afraid of disturbing them further. Some of them are even considered dangerous. But now we'd like to try an experiment. Maybe you can get through where we have failed. It's worth a try, if you'll do it."

"When do you want me?"

"Tomorrow afternoon will be fine, if that's convenient for you."

"I'll bring my accompanist. You just supply the piano and the audience and we'll surely try to reach them."

The major left and I had another show to do. At about three o'clock in the morning, when I was in bed, it suddenly hit me! Tomorrow I was going to a mental institution! I had once been a patient in a mental institution . . . and now I was going back to one.

I stared into the blackness above me and felt my body stiffen. Perspiration began to form between my shoulder blades. I hadn't felt this way since . . . since before I had committed myself to that institution . . . over ten years ago. My nerves and muscles were remembering, just as my mind was remembering. I tried to relax, taking deep and even breaths, matching Burt's sleeping rhythm in the other twin bed.

I was well, I told myself, and had been for years. There was nothing to fear. Besides, my mental breakdown had been due to alcoholism, my mind had given way just as my body had. I was healed now because I hadn't had a drink in years.

And yet, had my breakdown really been due to drinking? Might I not have wound up in Bloomingdales even if I'd never taken a drink? That question had haunted me for years. Now I faced it with a new urgency.

If drink had not been the cause of my mental illness, then I wasn't safe now from another breakdown. The rigidness of my muscles right now, the cold sweat that was breaking out all over my body, the paralyzing lock of my jaw, the rapid pulse, were these the beginning symptoms of another illness?

No, I told myself. No! This was nothing but an attack of nerves. It hadn't started like this before. But what *had* been the symptoms, then? What had I seen and how had I felt? I had always shut away those memories but now I wanted to know again, to remember.

I tried to recall the various bleak furnished rooms I had existed in, drinking a quart of whiskey a day and another quart each night. Consciousness was a fleeting thing, and with it came the spiders . . . soft and furry ones as large as rats. They clung to the walls about my bed and hypnotized me with bulging, red-rimmed eyes. Sometimes they would change, dissolve into faces that were human but inhuman, sticky with hair, slack, dripping mouths, milk-colored eyes. Then the faces would break apart into a thousand pieces, each piece a bug with long pincers. They swarmed over me. I slapped at them, clawed at my body, but there was no escaping them. They were eating me alive.

With a physical effort I wrenched my mind away from those memories. It had been years ago, but they were as vivid as ever, and perhaps dangerous. A non-active alcoholic, no matter how long he has been dry, is only an arm's length away from again being drunk. Perhaps a reversion to mental illness was as close, or even closer. Perhaps all we had to do was wander down the wrong corridors of the mind, and open the wrong door. My fear brought on the physical symptoms in mounting degree.

I reached over and snapped on the bed lamp. I think I half expected to find myself in the narrow room of the hospital, a room with a single barred window, but instead a warm pink glow filled the hotel room to reveal the familiar things I traveled with—my gowns and luggage, my dog asleep at the foot of my bed, and my husband nearby. Burt stirred but didn't waken. I was glad of that. He had been through so much with me and I didn't want him to think it was going to start all over again.

I had an obligation to Burt, and to myself, an obligation not to take chances. Certainly visiting a mental hospital would be a dangerous thing. Let some other performer entertain those men, someone who was safer. I'd call the major first thing in the morning and cancel the engagement.

I switched off the light and pulled the covers under my chin. But sleep wouldn't come. Something gnawed at me and would give me no rest. This thing, an inner voice, said, "What's the matter, Lillian, have you lost your courage? You claim you're well but you're afraid to test it? If that's the case, then you're not as strong as you pretend to be. You're running away, Lillian, and that won't solve anything. Oh, how well you should know the futility of running from a problem."

I turned on my stomach and pulled the pillow over my head, but nothing could muffle the voice. It continued, "And what of the men in that ward? Think of those living with dead minds. What if your singing can get through to them, give them a moment of pleasure, of reality? Can you deny them a chance for that?"

At last I murmured, "Okay, okay. I'll go there tomorrow." That decision was somehow comforting. I went to sleep.

The next afternoon, an Army car arrived to pick me up and take me to the hospital. My accompanist and I got in the back seat, a sergeant drove us. I had vowed that I'd go through this experience as if it was just another show, singing the same songs and sprinkling them with some light humor. But now that the trip had started I knew that I had fooled myself. I was on my way to a mental hospital and I couldn't forget it for a moment. I began to watch my reactions, waiting for symptoms, waiting.

I remembered the drive to the mental institution on the day of my own commitment. I remembered how I felt about the car and the driver. In those days I thought I was full of electricity, possessed a powerful current with which I could control others. Whenever I rode in a car I had the delusion that the driver was under my control, that he was doing exactly what my mind told him to do. I'd watch traffic and warn him of the danger spots; I'd tell him when to slow down and when to speed up, when to turn, when to honk his horn. And, miraculously, he obeyed me. Or so I thought. Actually, I did not say a word.

It was the same when I rode a plane, or a train, or a ferry boat; the pilot or the engineer was always under the control of my electrical thought waves. There were times, of course, when the man at the helm turned left when I told him to turn right, and those were times when I thought the electricity was so strong within me that it was pulling me out of my orbit, in an opposite direction from what I desired. At such times I was afraid to step into a tub of water, convinced that my current would ground and I'd be electrocuted.

I remembered one such period when I went to a dance with a young man and I could not follow him. I apologized to him, explaining, "I'm sorry but I'm not dancing very well because of the electricity. The magnetism is holding my feet to the ground and I can hardly lift them."

He grinned at me and said, "Sure."

"No, really. I'm full of electricity tonight. That's why I have slacks on, you see, to conceal the sparks around my ankles."

Laughing out loud he said, "You don't have to convince me you're a hot number. You've got sparks all over you, not just at the ankles."

I remembered all this now as I rode behind the sergeant. Testing my powers, I sent him a mental message to speed up. He ignored it. My second message told him to turn right. He ignored that one, too. I smiled to myself. The sergeant wasn't having any of my electricity today. The circuit was closed. But I continued to be on the alert, watching myself closely.

The major met us at the door of the hospital, introduced us to members of his staff, then led us down a long corridor. The windows were narrow and barred, just as mine had been. We stopped before a double door and the major said, "Your audience is in there, Miss Roth. Good luck."

I burst through the double door, threw up my arms in greeting and called out, "Hy, fellows."

There was silence—a silence that exists only in a room like this. It wasn't the kind of eager, "hear a pin drop" silence of an average audience during a good performance. No, this was the silence of nothingness. There were sixty men in the room, but not one of them was really there. They were off in their own secret, nebulous worlds. They had front-row seats in a vacuum.

Some were gray-haired men, veterans of the first World War, others were hardly more than boys, casualties of Korea. They sat in rows of chairs before me, most of them with their heads down, eyes on the floor. Here and there a man held his head up to stare fixedly past me at the blank wall, seeing the vision that was always with him, engraved on the retina of his eyes. One or two grinned, child-like, at something not visible. Each man was an island, and wracked by an impenetrable loneliness. I looked down the silent rows and my heart hurt for them. My eyes blurred for their unshed tears.

My pianist must have seen that I had forgotten my in-introduction speech because he went into the opening chords of my first song. I gave that song everything I had, and everything is pretty loud, I can tell you. When I finished—silence. No one had even moved.

I was at a complete loss. My regular night-club patter suddenly seemed terribly inane. The music led me into the second song. In the middle of that song I suddenly stopped. I waved my accompanist to silence, then walked close to the men and said, "I'll bet you fellows think I'm real stupid. I must look real silly standing up here waving my arms around. Go on, now, admit it. And you know something? I feel real stupid standing here because I know you don't really want to hear me sing. You think I'm just making a lot of unnecessary noise. Do you know something else? A few years ago I felt just like you do, and I was in a place just like this, and I didn't see anybody I loved and I wondered where they were."

Standing around the edge of the room were the nurses and doctors. I motioned toward them and said, "I know how you feel about the nurses, too. They're fine people and God bless them, but they can't always understand how you feel. You ask for a drink of water and they'll tell you that you just had one. Or if your tooth aches, they'll tell you it's nothing but nerves. I had a toothache when I was in an institution and they told me it was my imagination. But I knew the ache was there, even if they wouldn't believe me, and night after night I cried in agony. Finally I got them to take an X-ray of my mouth, and by gosh, I had an abscess. So I know how wrong they can be about us sometimes.

"What I want to say to you is that you shouldn't make me feel useless up here, because I'm one of you. Now, let's have some fun together, even if those doctors and nurses don't understand and sometimes look silly to us."

I launched into another song and before I had finished the refrain a blond, curly head which had been bowed low in the front row came up slowly. The face was young and blue eyes looked at me, not past me, but *at* me. I winked at him and something tugged ever so slightly at the corner of his mouth. It was such a poor little smile, but to me the most wonderful expression I had ever seen.

Behind him another head was lifted, and then another, and another! Suddenly, a balding man stood up and began to make a speech. I stopped the song to listen to him. Words tumbled out, formless and unintelligible. I found out later he had not spoken in fifteen years and was going to have to learn all over again how to form words. But it made no difference. I became so excited I clapped my hands and made a speech right back at him, my words no more intelligible than his, I'm sure. But what did the words matter? We were communicating. He had left his island!

I decided to go ahead and do the part of my night-club act in which I choose dancing partners from the ringside tables. When the speechmaker paused for breath, I cried out, "How about dancing? Anybody want to dance with me?"

Several hands came up waveringly. I gently touched one young man by the hand and led him to the open floor while the piano began to pound out a syncopated beat. That boy began to move, slowly at first, then with increasing confidence. My! How he could dance! And when we finished there was applause, scattered and ragged, but applause! Now a line had formed, about ten men waiting to dance with me. We waltzed and fox-trotted and even tried the rumba and the mambo. From time to time I'd catch the faces of the doctors and nurses around the edge of the room and their expressions were of happy incredulity.

After dancing with the last man in line I said, "Gee, if this is a party, where are the refreshments?"

Cakes and cookies and tea were brought into the room and we all adjourned to the buffet table. For the next fifteen minutes we stood around and talked. Not everybody talked, of course, but many of them did. The curly-headed boy, the first one to look up at me when I told them I had been in a hospital, kept following me around. He lacked the courage to come directly up to me, but I was certain he wanted to say something. I later learned he was a Korean vet and since his hospitalization five years before had been absolutely mute.

I turned to him and said, "Hello there."

He blushed and looked at the floor. Then slowly, with a great effort of will, he brought his eyes back up to mine. "Miss Roth," he said in a low, strained voice. "You were sick?"

"I was sick, just like all of you."

"And . . . you got well?"

"I did."

"Will you do me a favor?"

"Of course I will."

"Will you write my mother and tell her you saw me? And would you tell her that I'm going to get well, too?"

I nodded my head. I couldn't speak.

On the drive back to my hotel it suddenly occurred to me that all during the party with the men in the ward I hadn't once thought about myself. I had forgotten to stand aside and observe my own symptoms. I had completely shed the fears I had lived with since my own hospitalization. The shadows no longer reached for me.

The man who made the speech, the curly-headed boy, all the men I had danced with . . . for that hour, we had made each other whole. I'm sure that is God's plan, that we should help each other, that we should find His goodness and strength in our fellow-men when we give of each other.

11
The Turn of the Road

As I climbed slowly back to the top of the night-club circuit, as my pay went up from one thousand to five thousand a week, and finally to twelve thousand, I was, of course, pleased that I had made the comeback all the way. Yet I discovered it wasn't all the way, after all.

I had not overcome some of my personality flaws. Some of my worst faults were still with me and could not be banished by twelve thousand dollars a week, or twelve times that.

A Japanese philosopher once said, "The same devils ahead are the same devils behind." My personal devils still lurked around each turn of the road, no matter what high ground I reached.

I never felt completely secure or wanted. On a night when the audience would respond warmly to my performance and I'd leave the stage in a storm of applause, my trip to the dressing room would be like a journey on a cloud. But the moment I closed the dressing-room door and was alone, everything would become unreal and I'd begin to worry that tomorrow night there would be no applause, no affection or acceptance from the audience.

Then the old sense of melancholy and loneliness would get hold of me again. How strange that all day long I could be surrounded by people, in fact often be the center of their attention and the object of their praise, and still feel lonely. I suppose it is partly due to the fact that people often over-estimate me, think I'm wiser or better than I am, and so I'm all alone with my true self.

Being lonely, I can sense it in others. Sometimes at night in a club I can look across the room and see a stranger seated at a table and at once I feel a constriction around my heart. The droop of his shoulders, something about his demeanor, the forlorn attitude tell me that he is lonely. I often have an urge to go up to him and speak to him, touch him, but I never do, of course. We cannot invade another's wilderness. That man may have a good reason for his melancholy. But why am *I* so desolate? In the midst of seeming success and fame and a degree of fortune, why is there an ache inside me? For my mother? For the child I can never have? For a father loved but understood too late? For hurts inflicted? For things undone? I don't know. I don't know.

Another personal devil that continues to lurk on the

road ahead is my temper. I've worked hard to overcome its trigger quickness and I think I've made some progress, but not enough. I'm not seeking perfection in that department, either. I just wish that I could be more patient with people. I'm impatient when they lack drive and purpose. Personally, I'm quick and intuitive in my actions (which certainly doesn't mean I'm always smart or correct), and when those around me seem to drag their feet, to vacillate, well, I'm apt to blow up. My blow-ups are fearful things and I'm always heartily ashamed of them. But afterwards, when I say I'm sorry—well, that doesn't always take away the hurt I've inflicted.

When strangers come up to me and tell me how strong and wise they think I am, I'm terribly embarrassed and feel that I should say, "Now look here, I'm moody and impatient and sharp-tempered. Inside me I still cry with old sorrows. You give me too much credit." But I never say it. I don't want to see their eyes hold disappointment.

I was now at the height to my night-club comeback, working fifty weeks out of the year, crisscrossing the country at a hectic rate. Yet I began to feel a persistent restlessness. True, I was one of the top night-club draws, but I knew this wasn't what I wanted for the rest of my life. After all, I was doing essentially the same act I had done for more years than I really wanted to count. There was no sense of challenge left. Through constant work I had made a comeback. I had regained assurance and I had lost my fear of delving into new fields.

At last I knew what I wanted to do with my life; I wanted to spend my mature years in a more fulfilling effort and finally become what I had started out to be in Hollywood when I was twelve years old—a straight dramatic actress.

I remember when I was in my teens, I had been asked by Jesse Lasky and Ernst Lubitsch to appear in *The Love Parade* with Maurice Chevalier. Oh, I remember my excitement at the chance to play a romantic role opposite such a personality. But when I arrived on the set I found I was to play the comedy lead. It was a terrible disappointment. As so often happens in Hollywood, I became typed. When Jesse Lasky suggested me for a part in *The Vagabond King*, I thought I could break out of the type, but the first day on the set the director took a look at me and moaned, "I asked for a Pola Negri and I get a Louise Fazenda. No . . . you'll never do for sex appeal." From that I went into Marx Brothers pictures. When I finally did win a straight dramatic role at Warner Brothers, playing with Barbara Stanwyck, the director decided to add a song to my part in the final scene and I did "If I Could Be With You One Hour Tonight." I was remembered for the song, not for my acting.

It's easy, when you're young, to go along and do what people think you should do. They said I could make people laugh, and I could make them feel good with my songs, and these were rare gifts. Perhaps so. But on the other hand, I don't think anyone deserves much credit for doing what comes naturally. But to be a serious actress, to create an entirely different character from what you are, there was a challenge!

It was a challenge I had waited twenty-seven years to meet!

Burt realized how I felt and as usual brought his calm logic to bear on the situation. He said, "You're on top now, Lillian. It took you—well, forty-six years and a lot of heartaches to get there. Are you certain you want to give up the monetary security?"

"We all want and need security. But how much more do I need?"

"There will be a big cut in income. They don't pay twelve thousand a week in the legitimate theater."

"I've got my annuity for my old age. I don't need so much money. What on earth would I use it for? You know I was never crazy about clothes. I don't go for jewelry. I use them only for my stage appearances. So what's all the money for? Burt, don't you understand . . ."

"Of course, I understand, but I just want you to go into this with your eyes wide open. You'll work harder and make less money and I want you to be certain in your own mind that this is what you really want."

"Yes," I admitted. "I'm willing to give up the big money. I'd like to do some dramatic TV shows, or summer stock. I'm ready to work hard, to learn from the ground up, but in the end I want to be a good actress. If, after an honest try, I don't think I have it, I'll be the first to admit it and I'll quit. Then I'll sit in the sun and grow roses."

Burt opened a campaign to land a good dramatic spot for me on a TV show. He informed my booking agents of my request, but nothing happened. My agents just couldn't believe I was serious. They had never had a client who voluntarily took a big cut in income, which also meant a big cut in their commissions. They stalled. To have come so far and still to have no control over my own destiny seemed unfair to me.

Well, I appeared on a few TV variety shows, on Ed Sullivan's show, with the Dorsey Brothers, Frankie Laine, and Arthur Murray. But naturally, I always had to sing. And I didn't feel that I showed up well on these shows. Things were done in such a rush, there were so many mechanical requirements that stood between me and contact with the audience. When you're accustomed to working intimately with the people in front of you, changing your timing or interpretation to suit their mood, you find televised variety shows a very frustrating medium.

Stand where the chalk mark is. Look toward this camera at this point. Then turn and look in this direction. Then step this way for a close-up. Turn for profile. Turn this way for full face. Watch the mike boom. Watch the conductor. Watch the camera lights. Watch the floor marks. Watch the clock . . . watch everything but the people you're singing to. Brother! I have the greatest admiration for those who have mastered the mechanics of TV and can appear to sing with intimacy, but it wasn't what I wanted. I wanted to be an actress, not a singer.

Then the break came. In November, 1955, I was offered the lead in "Outcast," a drama on the United States Steel Hour over CBS-TV. My first elation was tempered when I learned it was the part of an alcoholic. Wouldn't the public think I was capitalizing on my own past? Would they think that since I hadn't played my own part in the movie version of *I'll Cry Tomorrow* I was now trying to do it on TV, under a different title? Would they compare me with Susan Hayward? Would they say, "Oh, but it doesn't take any talent for *her* to play an alcoholic because she's been one?"

But even as I catalogued my misgivings I knew that I'd take the part. I wanted to act and here was my chance.

Actually, playing the part of an alcoholic was a challenge because a real alcoholic never knows what he looks like to other people. He just can't see himself objectively. And usually, when he is sober, it's too painful to observe other drunks, it brings back too many shameful memories.

I knew from experience some of the difficulties I would have in the drunk scenes. I had had a week in summer stock, playing the title role in "Anna Lucasta." I knew that I hadn't done my drunk scene in that play as well as I should have.

In Anna's first scene she comes into a bar and says to the bartender, an old friend, "Make it a gin—straight."

On the stage, of course, you're served water, but even so I had difficulty lifting that glass to my mouth.

Backstage, I spoke to the actor playing the bartender, "Please do me a favor. Be sure and check that glass every time before you give it to me. Someone might try to be funny and put some real gin in it. It has happened to me before."

"Don't worry, Lillian," he said, "it'll be nothing but H_2O."

I trusted him, yet at rehearsals I would feel a stiffness in my arm when I tried to raise the glass to my lips, and I'd always spill it. This is silly, I thought. When the curtain goes up on a regular performance I'll be all right. But I wasn't. The stage directions called for me to take the drink and "slug it down" in one gulp. On opening night I felt panic. I got it down but I choked in the process. It took me three performances before I could take that shot without breaking into a sweat, and a whole week before I managed to look and act like a normal alcoholic, if you can call an alcoholic "normal."

And in the last scene of the play I was supposed to be tipsy and very bright and gay. Oh, what a chore that was for me! My own drinking had never been bright and gay. It had been full of the blackest shadows. I wasn't pleased with the way that scene went. So when the role came along in the U. S. Steel Hour, I remembered all this, but I took the part.

In "Outcast" I played a successful woman motion-picture writer who began to drink, not heavily at first, but enough to annoy her husband, who left her. One night my child has a fever but I'm out on the town and when I come home it is too late to save the child's life. Out of this tragic loss comes my alcoholism, and I lose my job and my self-respect. My one remaining friend tries to help me but it is to no avail. I hire a maid with a small girl and this takes the place of my own lost child. I stay sober until the maid gets married and takes the child away, then I lapse back again to my heavy drinking and no one can help me. In the end I am saved by the sudden reappearance of the maid and the child and the new husband. They have heard of my trouble and now want me to come and live with them. Clasping the child to my bosom, I go off with my new-found family and, presumably, to sobriety.

When I appeared for the first rehearsal I was nervous and a bit diffident. Though I was the star, the rest of the cast was composed of professional actors and actresses who had made their marks in the theater and my regard for them was high.

We sat on folding chairs on a bare stage and had our first read-through. As the various voices put flesh and blood into the play, it began to assume reality. I read my part in the closing scene, where I embrace the child and go happily off with my new family, off to sobriety and a fresh start in life. I read it through, and when I finished I felt something was wrong, something was radically wrong.

The lines did not come off. Of course, on the first read-through you're not supposed to give it too much interpretation, too much emotion. The reading is more to see and hear the skeleton of the play, and the director isn't going to expect much at this point. Still, I thought I had not only read it badly, but I had an awful conviction I would never read that scene any better.

I returned to my hotel that night in a state of depression. Burt recognized my mood at once but he was careful not to mention it. He knew from experience it was better to let me bring the problem into the open. We had a late supper in the dining room, took the doggies for a short walk, and then went up to our rooms where I paced the floor and smoked too many cigarettes. Burt watched television and pretended not to notice.

"Burt!" I finally broke out. "Burt, I was terrible in rehearsal today."

He got up and turned off the TV, resumed his chair, lit a cigarette and said, "It was the first reading, wasn't it?"

"Yes, but . . ."

"No buts. It was the first reading, period. You'll get into the part tomorrow all right, and you know it."

"That's what I keep trying to tell myself, but I don't really believe it. Something's wrong."

"You're keyed up, worried about your first big dramatic part, and no wonder. It will pass, Lillian. You'll give a good performance no matter how bad the rehearsals may seem to you."

"Damn it, Burt!" I shouted at him. "I'm sick of the pollyanna stuff. I tell you something was deeply wrong with my reading today and I don't know what it was. I can't put my finger on it."

Burt looked at me more searchingly now, taking me more seriously. "Did you read poorly all through the play, or just part of it?"

"The last scene, mostly. I . . . I just couldn't seem to get the feel of it. Maybe if I read it now, if you cued me, maybe it would help."

"You need sleep more than you need rehearsal," Burt said.

Ignoring his protest, I snatched up the play and leafed quickly through to the last scene. I began reading the scene half aloud, wondering what was wrong. What was it deep inside me that resisted this scene? Why couldn't I speak the words properly and with feeling?

Even now I was stumbling over the words. Then, with lightning-like illumination, I knew what was wrong.

"Burt . . . Burt!" I cried. "It's not me, it's not my fault. The scene just does not ring true."

"What do you mean by that?"

"The motivation is wrong. An alcoholic just wouldn't act the way this woman is acting. That was my trouble with the scene, it just went against the grain. And the more

I lived the part the more I couldn't bring myself to play this last scene."

"Maybe you're right."

"Well, follow my reasoning now and tell me if you don't agree. The story has this woman stop drinking as soon as she has someone to love. We know that isn't true, that isn't the way an alcoholic is constituted. Even if this woman had stopped drinking in order to be with the child, that would have been only enforced sobriety. Right?"

"You're right. And she would have resented that kind of sobriety, and eventually broken it."

"Exactly. And if, as the plot has it here, she went off to live with the child and its parents, it could only have been a temporary crutch, and she'd know it. She'd have a home and love, but in the end that wouldn't stop her drinking. This scene is wrong."

Burt said, "All right, let's think for a moment what that woman would really do."

"Since the child was taken from her once, she would never have the confidence that it would not happen again, and that she would not drink again. She has not found the solution to her problem."

Burt smiled. "So she joins our Alma Mater, the A.A."

"Yes, in time, perhaps," I added, "but the outcome is not certain."

"Well," said Burt, "why don't you talk to the director

and the writer. After all, you are an expert on the alcoholic question."

I did not think it was my province to meddle in the writing, but Burt insisted that I talk to them about my thoughts.

When I told my feelings to the director the next day, he was eager for me to expand on the subject. The writer agreed and changed the end to fit the realities of alcoholism. In the body of the play, I had a friend who was a member of A.A., and this friend inferred that he would come to me any time he was needed. So, in the new final scene, which was played entirely in pantomime, I am alone in the empty house. I had refused to go with the child and parents to their home, knowing such an arrangement will not stop my drinking, knowing that I will only bring disgrace and heartache to those I love.

Now I am alone. My furniture has been repossessed, my friends have left, my career is finished, my sanity is on the verge of cracking. There is nothing but a great emptiness all about me. What point is there to life? Where is any hope? I move about the empty apartment, forsaken, stricken, fighting the silent hysteria that is within me. There is a telephone still connected; it stands on a packing crate. With trembling hands I call the man who promised to come if I ever needed him. I say, "I'm waiting for you."

At dress rehearsal I lived this woman's life so completely and emotionally that when it came to the final scene I was so hysterically gagged up I could just barely get those words out—"I'm waiting for you."

At the end of the rehearsal I found many people in tears: the rest of the cast, the stage hands, the camera and lighting crews. There's a saying in the theater that if you have a good dress rehearsal you'll have a poor opening performance. I thought that I'd never again be able to create that emotional mood.

During the actual performance I again lived the character, so intently, in fact, that I couldn't judge whether I had given a good theatrical performance or not. I knew that I had personally suffered the problem as if it had been mine to suffer again.

The minute the show was over, everyone in the cast crowded around to congratulate me. I was truly joyous under my tears. But I thought what will the TV and theatrical critics have to say about me?

Right after the show, Burt and I had to leave for a club date in Canada and as we piled into the car and headed north along the Hudson River, I said, "Tomorrow morning, when the reviews hit the newsstands, I'll either be glad I skipped out of town in the middle of the night, or else I'll wish I was back taking bows."

We turned on the radio to listen to the commentators, and shortly after midnight they began to talk about my performance on the U. S. Steel Hour! Barry Gray, Big Joe, and Jack Eigen all said I had given a moving performance.

Still, what would the newspaper critics say, I wondered. I had received reviews all my life, but this time it was really crucial. I had embarked on a new career. I had taken my first step as a dramatic actress. What would the verdict of the profession be?

It was two days before we got the New York papers up in Canada. It was worth the wait. Jack O'Brian, who can be very caustic and is a no-holds-barred critic, wrote in the New York *Journal-American* that I had given a "walloping performance." Ronald Lindbloom had in the past given me many a nice review of my club work, and now wrote in the Newark *Evening News* that I was "a top candidate for an Emmy Award for the year's best piece of dramatic acting." And Jack Gould, in the revered New York *Times*, wrote as follows:

"Lillian Roth gave a magnificent portrayal of an alcoholic in 'Outcast,' an original drama presented last night on the United States Steel Hour over Channel 2. In its understanding, in its poignancy, in its sensitivity, her performance was one that can only be called memorable . . . To the characterization of the drunk she brought a haunting reality. The slovenly speech, the loudness and furtiveness of the woman's behavior, the loneliness and fear that cannot be explained, all these she etched into an unforgettable portrait. The closing scene of the play, when the alcoholic woman picks up the phone to seek help and promises that this time she will really try to help herself, was as gripping and moving a moment as television has

[237]

had in a very long time. Miss Roth was an inspired woman last night and also a great artist. . . ."

I thought, foolishly, that my dramatic career had been launched. After these notices (the other reviewers were just as enthusiastic) I'd be in demand and could pick my shows and my stories. It would be a breeze.

But it wasn't. Again, we had run into a snag. The critics had accepted me, the audience had liked my performance, but the agents put a damper on my enthusiasm.

Burt came home one day and looked at me with a serious face. "I guess we can forget about serious dramatic shows for a while," he said.

"Why?"

"We couldn't accept them. You're all booked up in clubs."

"For how long?"

"The rest of 1956."

"Burt . . . next year, so help me . . . !"

"Sure, Lillian, next year will be different."

The following year was to be different, but the change was brought about in a curious way. Something happened that should have strengthened my agents' hands in the struggle to keep me in clubs, but the result was the reverse. What started out to be just another night-club engagement turned into something quite different.

In January 1957, I was booked into the "Persian Room" of New York's Plaza Hotel for a return engagement. I had been warmly received there the year before, but I was not sure whether this year the audience would show the same enthusiasm. However, they welcomed me back in a heart-warming manner on opening night and after all the years of night-club work I still felt a surge of excitement.

It was short-lived, as usual, as I began again all my old misgivings. "Tonight was fine, but what about tomorrow night?"

Two days later, when I was out shopping, I telephoned Burt at the hotel. He answered me with a question, "Have you seen *Variety* yet?"

"No," I said. "Why?"

"Get a copy and read your review."

"What does it say, Burt?"

"Just get a copy," he said and hung up.

I left the phone booth and took a cab to the hotel, pausing on Broadway to pick up a copy of *Variety*. I felt a small knot of fear in the pit of my stomach as I flipped through to the page where my act was reviewed. I began to read and couldn't believe my eyes. I skipped from paragraph to paragraph, saying aloud to myself, "No . . . no . . . oh my goodness . . . no!"

The cabbie turned around, looked at me quizzically, and said, "What's the matter, lady? You keep saying 'no' every time I make a turn. Don't you think I know my way to the Plaza? I've been driving for thirty years."

I assured him that my exclamations had nothing to do with his driving skill. I folded up the paper and when I finally arrived back in my hotel room, I felt like a kid with a report card full of A pluses. I whirled Burt about the room and I kept saying, "I've done it. I've done it. I've finally won 'freedom from sympathy.' "

I sat down to read that review again, and I like to quote from it, not for the reason of self-glorification, but simply because of the important role it was to play in my life.

"Racking up a return date in a four weeker at the poshy room, well past Phase 1 of a comeback launched so resoundingly in the not-too-long-ago postwar, Lillian Roth is one of the heartthrobbing encores in show biz. Not a comeback in the traditional 'gotta get back in harness' sense, but a smashing personal rehabilitation bespeaking the kind of class in the human race that becomes special and overpowering because of the rarity thereof . . .

"When a 'comeback' performer can make the circuit a second and third time around, it's no comeback any more —it's a going regular force, and entity apart from the human interest values that were originally bound up in the long road back to the realities. That being so, the 'this is your life' pitch no longer applies. Miss Roth's twilight period is over with. Period. She has to be judged strictly on performance. This is how a Lillian Roth would undoubtedly want it. Want it or not, this is what she gets. What she gets is one word: Greatness.

"Miss Roth can still belt 'em; but even if she couldn't live it up on the chateroos, she'd knock 'em dead on the delivery, special handling, registered and personal. This is a La Roth '57 from whom many a latterday thrush-in-a-rush can take lessons and who would be glad, or should be glad, to have what the four star girl of H'wood back-when and the two A's of more recent vintage has forgotten. What she has forgotten is almost nil, but even little favors would be welcome, or should be welcome, to most of today's crop of canaries who can hardly make it without a disk attachment.

"Miss Roth made it in the days when you hadda say something 'with nothing' like the gadgets, echo chambers, electronic 'new sounds' and make-'em-look-better editing devices of the Post WW II era. Like the rest, she may have been enhanced in the throat stuff by the west coast soundtracks, though she was never one to be too fastidious about shouts and growls; but she also notched scores and accolades in vaude and musicomedy where the product, if it is spurious, becomes all too evident to the public—but quick—and only jen-you-wine articles could hit the heavy paydirt.

"In the athletic sweepstakes, the legs go first, the noodle and knowhow remain. In the singing arena, the pipes fade long before the savvy is ready to check out, if it ever does. Miss Roth not only retains the savvy but the years have improved it; and the personality and the individuality, the trademarks of style, are undoubtedly at or near peak. So, while a lot of her career is behind her, there's plenty ahead of her, because that is the way Miss Roth is endowed. Add to these a mccoy modesty, a manner of self-effacement and ribbing that are good by themselves and, in the commerce of show biz, represent a fillip to an 'act.' Miss Roth's 'new act' is almost as good as the old one—pre A.A. version. But even half that much of Roth brand is terrific. What's more, she looks great, behaves ditto, and is as girlish as she used to was without being skittish . . .

"Not many performers, whatever their stature, can top Miss Roth on the evergreens she helped make standards or beat her to the tape on any of the songs they sang in her era and that she would latch onto in a doing-what-comes-naturally. Whether it's 'World On A String' or 'How Deep Is The Ocean,' these are pitched to reflect the lyrics and the meaning rather than the pitcher, which is another something that many thrushes don't learn when they are more anxious to front a 'style' regardless of the tune at hand. She whams over 'Sing You Sinners' like she had the copyright, and doesn't use a battering-ram on the long line of standards to which she had such a boxseat.

"She can be ultra-humorous, too, as in the very clever 'Sam,' and her special material isn't merely something she's paid for but a reflection of what can be done when a Roth wants to break out of the norm and into the rarefied atmosphere of an 'arrangement' that so often misses fire . . .

"And who but Lillian Roth can get away with a community-sing 'Let Me Call You Sweetheart'? She's also the hep and happy kid on the chatter and patter and makes a customer feel she wouldn't 'descend' to memorizing a script. She hoofs it with the ringsiders, which at the Wednesday preem hardly hinted at anything but pushbutton spontaneity . . .

"Finally, there's the exit production, 'Please Tell Me When.' It's a beaut in her file and cannot be topped. So this leaves her without phony begoffs and without an encore. If it isn't sensational as a finale, it's preciously close. The crowd is just overcome. Short of leaving 'em limp, what more can be expected of a singer?   *—Trau*"

One phrase from the review ran through my head: "She has to be judged strictly on performance." At last I had outgrown the attention based on curiosity; at last I was being judged strictly as a performer. I felt free from a long bondage.

"Burt," I said, "now is the time to quit. How much higher can I go? Now let's plan for the future. How much longer am I booked in clubs?"

"February in Florida, March in Cuba, and on April 2 you open for a month at the Sahara Hotel in Las Vegas."

"That's the last?"

"So far."

"Well, that's it, then. Call my agents and tell them

[*243*]

they'd better open a dramatic department because otherwise they're losing a singer. Las Vegas will be the last one."

I imagine I sounded very firm and full of confidence to Burt, but inside I was trembling. For this was the very first decision I had ever made on my own in my entire life.

12

The Two Faces of Cuba

Success is such an elusive thing. When you think you've finally got it in the palm of your hand, it can slip away, evaporate like a cloud of steam. After that review of my act in *Variety*, I had the comfortable conviction that I had it made. I didn't presume that I would be a smash hit every time I got up on the stage to sing, on the other hand I thought that never again would I have real difficulty. But then came Cuba!

In Havana I was to call upon all the skills I had learned over the years, but they weren't enough. What started out to be a gay and triumphant farewell tour turned into a near tragedy.

Strange about my going to Cuba in the first place. I have never had a great desire to leave the United States for bookings abroad. Several years ago I had offers from

London and the Continent, and under the pressures of my agents and managers I said I might go. But I never did. I never signed the contracts. It's not that I'm a provincial, not that I'm uninterested in other peoples, it's just that there has always been so much at home I had missed, still had to see and experience, that I didn't feel the need to go far afield.

I must confess that my little doggies had something to do with it. You often have great trouble taking pets into and out of foreign countries and I was determined not to be separated from them. I've smuggled them into hotels, planes, trains, and night clubs, but smuggling them past customs inspectors of a strange land is something else again.

But my reluctance to accept the foreign offers was due primarily to my belief that there is a right time for everything. When I didn't go to London, I felt that it wasn't the right time for me to go to London. The Lord moves in a mysterious way, but sometimes, if we listen, look, and think very carefully, we can see the pattern he intends for our lives and then we don't push and strain to try and alter it.

However, the Cuban engagement eventually seemed to fall into the proper pattern. I was to appear there for ten days, starting February 9, then to Las Vegas, and my career as a night-club entertainer was ended. Cuba would be my first appearance outside the U.S.A. and perhaps it would also be appropriate for my farewell.

That January, while I was still appearing at the Plaza in New York, my agent called to say that the Cuban club, the *Montmartre*, wanted to cancel my engagement. Two feelings rushed through me. First, I thought, "Ah, I'm so glad. I was never quite sure about the correctness of going there, and now I can take a rest before winding up my career at Las Vegas." But almost immediately the second reaction set in: "Oh my goodness! They don't think I'm box office. They think I'm slipping. They're wrong and I've got to show them they're wrong!"

Even at this stage of my life all the old insecurities returned; I still needed to get in there and prove myself just one more time. Also, I had spent considerable money for Spanish musical arrangements and Spanish costumes just for this one engagement, and it didn't seem right for them to cancel without giving any reason.

I paced my hotel room, torn between wanting to give up and wanting to fight. I looked at my new Spanish wardrobe, and maybe it was a typically feminine reaction to think, oh what a waste.

The gowns were vibrant and dashing. I had had them made up in colors that would catch the Cuban eye, reds and greens, and bright colors I don't ordinarily use on stage. They were off the shoulder with long torsoes, and one of the brilliant red ones had a black lace mantilla with a sprinkling of rhinestones. I thought if I don't go to Havana, I'll have to get a year of TV color shows to wear all these gowns.

[*249*]

Naturally, I wanted to know why they were trying to cancel my appearance.

One of the owners of the *Montmartre* came to New York to explain. The man who appeared at my hotel room was named Mario, six feet tall, dark, dashing, and charming. Just a woman's dream of a romantic Latin. He had his wife with him and she was one of the most beautiful women I had ever seen.

"Miss Roth," Mario said with a serious face, "there is trouble brewing in our country again."

"What kind of trouble?" I asked, as if I didn't know. The newspapers had been full of it.

"Well, arms have been smuggled in."

"Oh, you mean another revolution? Or is it the same one still going on against Batista?"

He seemed to wince. "I do not give it names. I do not call it revolt or liberation, but I know there is going to be some more shooting. Already there has been some—in the club!"

"You mean right in the *Montmartre?*" Burt demanded.

Mario nodded somberly. "The public investigator, he is something like your FBI, was shot and killed in the *Montmartre* two weeks ago. And his aid was killed with him. The police closed the place for a time."

"But it has reopened?" Burt said.

"It is open," Mario conceded, "but . . . well, it is a very easy place to get shot."

"What you mean is," I said, "you want to cancel my contract for my own good? In order to protect me?"

He shrugged his shoulders.

Now, I'm a funny person. When somebody tries to scare me off, I may well get scared but I pull a switch, I just get more determined. If the *Montmartre* was open and doing business, I could see no reason to let them out of my contract. I said as much.

"Miss Roth," Mario pleaded, "things are so unsettled down there. Please think of yourself and, well, wait for at least a month. Come in March instead of next month. It will be much better, believe me."

I agreed to the postponement, but not to the cancellation. I was going to wear that red dress with the long bodice, which would probably start a revolution of its own.

We juggled my schedule around so that when I left New York I went into the *Monte Carlo* in Miami Beach for my third return, and then, on March 5, I took a plane for Havana.

Four turbo-jet Rolls Royce engines rushed me through blue skies to the island in the blue water. When I landed, I was swept up in a frenzy of excitement: flash bulbs popping, reporters shouting questions, radio and TV men elbowing for a position near me, a hubbub of sound that became one thundering voice. In my faltering, dictionary-learned Spanish, I said, *"Buenos dias. Mucho gusto . . .*

glad . . . *alegre* . . . *contento. Gracias, gracias.*" How
pleasing it was to be greeted so affectionately, to be welcomed in a strange land as if you were an old friend.

Everyone grinned in happy satisfaction at my broken
Spanish and I was whisked off to customs. From there I
was introduced to a miniature car, already loaded with
my luggage, and squared and folded into a flat package
and stowed with the suitcases. Off we careened through
the countryside, but not fast enough to avoid seeing pain.
A sad-faced, emaciated cow was tied tightly by the throat
to a tree, foam dripped from her parched mouth, the rolling eyes begging for a quick end to agony. Nor was the
cow the only living thing that suffered. Naked children
scattered from the dusty highway. Men and women,
bent and aged beyond their years, scratched at the sun-
baked earth with primitive instruments. The poverty-
stricken appearance of the countryside stunned me.

Then all this was swept from before my eyes and in its
place rose a splendid city full of cars, shops, and modern
buildings, with all the trappings of civilization—Havana.
And in another moment I was in my hotel room, deep-
carpeted and ornately furnished, with windows that
looked out upon the limitless sea. Cuba seemed a paradox
of poverty and luxury.

That afternoon, I went shopping and saw another face
of Cuba. Everywhere I went, the streets were choked
with vivid flashes of color to dazzle the eye: red scarves,

scarlet dancing slippers, multicolored bandanas. And the sounds: bongo drums, castanets, jangling bracelets, and guitars to accompany the sweet, haunting voices. Everywhere was music and excitement. I discovered something about the Cubans that afternoon: it always seems to be holiday time in this sun-washed land, always a time of gaiety, of play, of celebration. And just as this thought crossed my mind there was a rattle of gunfire down the street. For a moment my holiday mood deceived me into thinking it was the sound of firecrackers, but the angry roar of army motorcycles disillusioned me at once. A block away there had been another political assassination. The crowd around me paused to turn impassive faces at the quick parade of military vehicles, then resumed its talking, laughing, singing, bargaining, gambling. Life was cheap, and death did not interrupt the living. But I had suddenly lost my appetite for all this and I hailed a taxi to return to my hotel.

My cabbie spoke English and I questioned him about the shooting. He was evasive, assured me it was probably nothing. Sure, people talked about revolution, he said, but there was nothing to it. I directed him to stop at a newsstand for a paper, somehow forgetting that I couldn't read them. There was a bold-face announcement across the top of the paper and I held up the Spanish words for my driver to read.

"What does it say?" I demanded.

"It is nothing," he said, waving the paper aside.

I put it back in front of his nose. "Read it to me, please."

He shrugged his shoulders and read, " 'Anyone shot after dark cannot hold the government responsible.' " He shrugged again and said, "You see? Nothing."

Burt had come to Cuba a couple of days ahead of me to make all the arrangements and now he kept telling me to relax and get into the right frame of mind for the evening's opening performance. I tried to relax, but it wasn't easy. There was something about the atmosphere in town that set my nerves singing. Beneath the color and gaiety there was a tension, an apprehension that showed in the people's eyes at unguarded moments. Colonel Batista, the "strong man" of Cuba, was going to need all his strength to keep the lid on this bubbling pot, I thought.

I arrived at the *Montmartre* at about seven o'clock, and it was decidedly after dark. I was struck at once by the sullenness of the doorman and then a similar mood on the part of the elevator operator. It was more than sullen; there was an attitude of suspicion and resentment. I walked into the club's gambling room, actually two tremendous rooms opening into each other. A babble of voices washed over me. The roulette, crap, and blackjack tables filled the middle of the room; on one side was an enormous bar at which five hundred people could stand, and on the other side of the second room was the stage.

At the moment, an enormous gambling wheel was set up on the stage.

The place was jammed with people and my first reaction was relief. I can draw them in a strange country, too, I thought. But slowly I began to realize that this wasn't the case at all. The people who were playing bingo and roulette had just wandered in off the streets, and they were reinforced by the busboys, the waiters, and the kitchen help. It seemed that everyone in town stopped at this time, not to see me, but to play bingo. And then I remembered something else: there had been no advertisements in the newspapers for my show. Nor had the management come to meet me and welcome me as is usually the case when you come to a club the first day. Mario had been so friendly up in New York, so much a gentleman; where was he now? Nobody seemed to be aware of my existence.

As I looked around the room and listened to the talk I realized, with a sinking heart, that this was strictly a Cuban club; there wasn't a tourist, a North American, present. If they listened to me at all they wouldn't understand my act, wouldn't understand the nostalgia, the new beat, the humor, the timing. I felt very small and lost.

That night, going backstage, I stepped into bedlam. There was nothing but a long, long tunnel that led to the kitchen. Waiters were bumping into each other and cursing; Cuban chorus girls, bosoms bare, were struggling into costumes; the bandsmen were adding weird sounds from their instruments as they tuned up; wardrobe women, cleaning women, stagehands, lighting men, and soundmen were all gesticulating and yelling at the tops of their lungs. I'm a pretty bombastic person myself, but before this I felt like a delicate and swooning belle from the Old Southland.

Somehow I found my dressing room. A dressing room? It was a canvas tent! It shut out neither sound nor people. All the time I was trying to dress, people kept barging into the tent, looked at me for a moment, regardless of my state of undress, then turned and walked out. I think that half of Cuba must have visited me in this manner, and each time my *"Buenas"* became weaker and weaker.

Through the canvas walls of my dressing room I heard my musical cue and I rushed on stage. In my absence the audience had changed; the busboys and dish washers had gone back to their jobs and now the regular Havana night-club crowd filled every inch of space in the vast room. I searched the faces anxiously; they were all golden in color, all Cuban, and in their language I could say little more than *"Buenas noches."*

I spoke my opening lines in an exaggerated manner, as if they were all lip readers, then went into the first song, "It's a Wonderful World." The song is fast and loud, but even so I couldn't drown out the buzz of conversation in that room. They just kept right on talking and gesturing and laughing loud. They looked at me while they talked, true, but it was all terribly disconcerting. And the waiters! I have never heard such bedlam from dishes and trays! There must have been a total of three thousand people jammed into that room, and every one of them seemed to be either yelling or banging dishes on a tray. It was as if the revolution had already started.

I plunged ahead with my act, singing my head off in a desperate effort to top the noise, to command their attention. Then, right in the middle of a song something happened that chills a performer's heart: about two hundred people suddenly stood up and walked out!

When people walk out on your act it's almost like a physical blow to the pit of your stomach and you don't seem to have any wind, or heart, left to go on. By walking out they have announced they find you so boring they can't stand you another minute. And those who don't walk out, well, even if they have liked you up to now they begin to revise their opinions. They say to themselves, "If those folks find her so boring, maybe I'm wrong in liking her. I guess I'd better not applaud very much for the rest of her act because it will show me up as not being very sophisticated."

No matter how hard a performer may try, he seldom recaptures an audience after a walk-out. Not that I had captured this one in the first place. But I tried—oh, how I tried! At the end, where I pass among the crowd to sing a song of farewell, they were just bewildered. They didn't know what I was doing. They called loudly for drinks or, if they stopped talking for a second, they stared at me open-mouthed.

After I bowed out of that room I raced down the long tunnel, bumping heedlessly into waiters and chorus girls until I came to my tent dressing room. I slammed into it, shaking the tent, knocking hangers to the floor. Nobody paid the slightest attention to me because I was just acting like all the temperamental Cubans. I sat before my dressing table, trembling. My farewell tour—was it to end like this? After forty years on the stage, they were beginning to walk out on me. Maybe I should have retired from night clubs ages ago.

Forgotten now was the applause over the years, the glowing reviews. Not the successes, but the humiliation in Cuba would be what I'd remember the rest of my life. I wished I was dead.

My face in the mirror looked worn and tortured. Then, behind it, I saw the hulking figure of a man. I swung toward him. He was a Cuban.

"I am the boss," he said.

"So what's your problem?" I asked.

"Just so you know who runs things."

"Do you run the noise, too? Where is Mario?"

"He is no longer the boss. I am the boss."

"Okay, then, why don't you boss those waiters of yours?" I cried.

"The waiters?"

"If you'll read the contract you have with me, you'll find there's not supposed to be any service during the last half of my act. Out there tonight it sounded like a boiler factory."

"People gotta eat."

"Feed them some other time, huh?"

He glowered at me. "I am the boss."

He left and I stared back at the face in the mirror. Well, I wasn't going to die tonight. I had my fighting spirit up.

Burt entered and sat down beside me.

"The show was awful, Burt," I said.

He shook his head. "It wasn't so bad. Believe me, darling."

I whirled on him, vent on him all my frustration and hurt. "Don't try to give me that business. I know the build-ups you always try to give me. Don't do it tonight. I know what happened out there. Two hundred people walked out on me. Don't you come in here and try to convince me I was a big hit. Please . . ."

We sat in silence for a time. At last I said, "Maybe we'd better go home."

"Try it one more night, Lillian."

"Is it going to be any better tomorrow? Am I going to be able to speak Spanish suddenly, or will they suddenly understand English? Is that big boss going to quiet the waiters all of a sudden?"

"I don't know, but it isn't like you to quit."

"What if they walk out on me again tomorrow? I don't think I could stand it, Burt."

"Try it just one more night, Lillian. I don't want you to leave Cuba remembering this."

"God knows I don't want to remember this as a farewell to my club career."

"Tomorrow night might be different. See if you can't stick it out."

"Burt, where's Mario? I haven't seen him since we arrived."

"I saw him this evening."

"But what's happened? This man who came in here . . ."

Burt frowned and I knew something had gone wrong, something beyond just my misery out on that stage. He seemed to choose his words carefully. "Mario is out."

"You mean he doesn't own the club any longer? He sold it?"

"Well, perhaps not exactly *sold* it. It's more that he surrendered it. Some sort of combine moved in on him and he just wasn't able to defend himself. I'm afraid that some very cute fellows now run the place. I don't like the setup at all. But . . ."

"Our contract was with Mario," I cried. "Don't you see? We can quit without breaking the contract, because we haven't signed a thing with the new owners."

Burt turned to face me directly. "Lillian, I don't want you to quit."

"They . . . they haven't threatened you, have they, Burt?"

He laughed. "You know how far anyone would get with me by threats. I've never asked you to do something that wasn't right for you, have I?"

This was true, of course. Burt had given me his heart and his mind a long time ago.

He said, "I think it's important for *you*. I want you to lick this thing. Otherwise it will haunt you."

I thought this place was already haunted, the way I had died on that stage. I finally said in a small voice, "All right. I'll give it one more chance. I don't see what can happen to change things, but I'll try. I'll try."

He patted my hand. "Better change and get back to the hotel."

"Burt . . . don't leave me."

"I won't."

"Stay with me every minute."

"Every minute," he nodded. "Now let's go to the hotel and get some sleep."

The next morning I awoke with the dull, flat feeling of failure. I dragged myself out of bed and into the shower, but that didn't revive me, it only chilled me. We ordered breakfast on the phone and when, about an hour later, it was wheeled into my room, the morning Havana newspapers were beside the coffeepot. I glanced at them, then took a second look. They all carried my picture. "Burt, look at this," I cried.

"You've got three front page stories," he announced. "Now if we can only find someone to translate them and see what they say . . ."

"I'm better off not knowing," I said.

But Burt called the waiter back and we found that he spoke English. He read the newspapers to us and they were reviews by the Havana critics, all of them rave notices of my performance the night before.

"But I don't understand. I don't understand," I kept saying. "It was terrible. The crowd didn't pay any attention to me, so how can these critics say that the performance was so great?"

"Well, maybe we were wrong in thinking . . ."

"We weren't wrong at all. You saw what happened."

Burt shook his head. "Well, all I know is that we've got a million dollars' worth of publicity in the morning papers. It may not make sense to you and me, but there it is. Let's be thankful that the critics liked you."

"But one of the critics said the audience loved me. How can he think that?"

"I don't know, Lillian. I just don't know how to figure it."

There was a knock on the door. Burt opened it and there stood Mario, the man I had originally signed the contract with, but who had since lost out. He swept into the room, took both my hands and kissed them.

"I did not get a chance to see you last night after the show. I tried but you had left."

THE TWO FACES OF CUBA

"Left—disintegrated!"

"It is of no consequence. I only wanted to add my own small word of congratulations. You were wonderful. You captivated them like no other performer I can remember appearing here."

I looked at Burt and he looked at me and then we both looked at Mario. "I'm beginning to feel like Alice in Wonderland," I said.

"Mario," Burt said, "Lillian was very upset because she never seemed to get through to the audience last night."

"But she did! She won their hearts."

"But they talked all through her act!" Burt gave him a puzzled look.

"Of course they did," Mario explained. "They were excited about her and they wanted to discuss it with each other. That's the way Cuban audiences are. When something pleases them they want to talk about it, share it with each other."

"Well . . . !"

"I sat in the audience and I heard what they were saying," Mario continued. "They were saying to each other, 'Isn't she wonderful?,' 'Isn't she great?,' 'Look at that beautiful dress and how good her figure is in it!' And when you danced with that young man, he came back to his table and said, 'Did you see me? Wasn't that a wonderful dance we did together?' And then for five minutes everybody at the table said how wonderful the dance was.

[263]

Oh, they adored you. The greatest reception they've given anyone as long as I can remember."

Burt was grinning now. But I said, "Wait just a minute. About two hundred people walked out in the middle of my performance. What about them? Did they think I was great, too?"

Mario looked puzzled for a minute, then his face broke into a broad smile. "Oh, them!"

"Yes . . . them!"

"They were part of a conducted tour. There were four hundred in the tour and they all demanded to see your show. But there wasn't room for all of them at once. So the tour split them up, let one half see the first part of your show, then took them out and let the rest see the second half."

Burt burst out laughing. "You see, Lillian. Now will you learn to stop jumping to conclusions."

I nodded. "Now I've heard everything."

Mario said, "Believe me that I do not exaggerate when I say that last night you were a triumph. I understand that reservations have been pouring into the *Montmartre* this morning. You'll fill that room for the entire time you're here."

How things can change between night and dawn. I was ashamed that my pride had overcome reason . . . ! Yet, I still had some misgivings. Mario was Cuban, he certainly knew the people. Okay, they liked me, but I hadn't communicated with that audience. I'd have to revise my material, cut out some of the humor, speak my lines slower, try to learn a few more Spanish words. There was the language barrier to make things more difficult. But there was also, I felt, a personality barrier. It wasn't enough for me that the audience liked me—I wanted to like them too, I wanted to know them, to understand them. I had misunderstood their behavior on opening night. They had been kind to me—I wanted to give them kindness in return.

When I arrived at the club that evening, I received further tangible proof of my success on the night before. The corpulent man who had called himself the "boss" in my dressing room, met me at the door of the *Montmartre* with a deep bow, his moonface all smiles.

"Ah, a great artiste, a great artiste, *señorita*. We are so honored."

"Thank you. I am sorry about yesterday," I said.

He shrugged with an apologetic smile. "Yesterday is of no importance. Today you are the toast of Havana. A great artiste."

"Well," I smiled, "enough toast to quiet those waiters during my great act?"

He bowed. "There will be no service of food or liquor during your act."

"And no clearing of dishes?"

He bowed again. "And no clearing of dishes. If any waiter makes a sound while you are on stage," he held

[*265*]

his enormous hands up before my eyes and slowly clenched them into fists, "I personally will break him in half."

That night we had quite a show. I had added a couple of Spanish words to my vocabulary. I greeted the audience by saying, *"Buenas noches, señors e señoras,"* and they applauded as if I had done something tremendous. Then I said in Spanish that I was happy to be with them this evening, and they cheered. When I announced my first song I said, *"Usta conta comigo,"* which was an invitation for them to sing it with me. And did they! We brought the roof down.

Then I began to realize that just as we think a foreign accent is cute, so they thought my Spanish was cute and they wanted to help me with it. Whenever I'd be stuck for a word, they'd call it out to me. The light men, the stage-hands, the orchestra, the audience, hundreds of them would shout the Spanish word and as a result I never could hear it quite right or say it properly, but they didn't mind at all. I'd just say, *"Si . . . si . . . gracias."* And that was enough for terrific applause.

And when it came to the dancing—well! I asked for a volunteer to teach me the Cha Cha Cha and up popped a thin Cuban with a grin larger than he was. Now, fortunately, I had spent some time back home trying to learn the Cuban rhythms, but I still hadn't mastered them. They have a certain beat that is quite difficult, with eight beats to the measure and then a certain kind of off-beat. It's six-two rather than our four-four. I'd done the American version of the Cha Cha Cha but it's nothing like they do it in Cuba. Anyway, this young man climbed onto the stage, and suddenly another man appeared with a set of bongo drums and began beating out the rhythm.

In the beginning, my partner and I stayed on opposite sides of the stage while he did a step and I'd repeat it. Slowly we got the same beat and then we came together for the end of the dance. As the applause rolled over us, an elderly Cuban jumped up on the stage. He wanted to do the Cha Cha Cha also, but he had an entirely different idea of it. He took out his handkerchief and did a donkey version where you pretend that the lady is a donkey and you have to whip her with the handkerchief to make her "go, go." That Cuban had gray hair, but there was nothing wrong with his wind. Ordinarily I dance with half a dozen people, but this night I danced with twenty, and they wanted more. The gaiety of the audience inspired me. I could have danced all night.

When it was time for my farewell song, they put a green spot on me instead of my usual pink one. You see, Cubans love green, and I love Cubans. So, resembling in color a billiard table, I made my way among the tables. The stagehands shouted directions at me and advice, and farewells. The audience was doing the same thing. We were all having a party together, everyone wanted to participate and have a good time.

In the days that followed, I became the object of a great

outpouring of affection by the Cuban people. Not only did they jam the *Montmartre* every night, but all during my visit they sent me gifts, cards, rosaries, and flowers, and whenever I appeared in the lobby of my hotel or on the streets, perfect strangers would come up to direct an explosion of Spanish at me, then grin and disappear. I didn't know what they said, not the exact words, but our hearts talked. We didn't have to know the same language to tell we liked each other. You can communicate, you can give love and respect and receive it back double even if there is not a single word you can speak in common. People are the same the world over, regardless of color, culture, or politics, and they will respond to each other if given the chance.

Regardless of the internal strife rampant in Cuba, the people remained warm and friendly, and I was sorry to leave them after my engagement was over.

But I was also pleased that I had heeded Burt's advice to "stick it out" after that opening night, for I had proved to myself that patience, kindness, and perseverance can work miracles. Had I not overcome my self-indulgent sensitivities, I would have made many enemies instead of winning a multitude of friends.

It was with high spirits that I rang for the porter and followed him and my luggage into the elevator. Perhaps I should have sensed that something was wrong by the way the porter and the elevator man talked to each other, for it was not with the usual volubility, rather in whispers, accompanied by furtive glances at me and the other passengers. I'm usually very sensitive to other people's moods, but this time I must have been insulated a bit by my own pleasurable feeling of success, for even in the lobby I failed to sense the tension of the people as they stood in small groups and talked with an altogether unnatural restraint.

I paid my hotel bill to a stony-faced cashier, then walked out of the lobby into the street . . . and there it was!

At the foot of the hotel steps, in a widening pool of blood, sprawled a young man. Standing in a semicircle about him were soldiers with drawn guns. In the distance, pedestrians hurried on their way with averted faces.

The young man was dead. I learned later that he was a university student and a few minutes ago had been leading a political demonstration against Cuba's strongman president, Colonel Batista. The soldiers had shot him down.

After the first hot flood of horror swept through me I thought, so young . . . so young! And then I thought once more about the paradoxical Cubans. They loved to sing and dance and make love and let problems wait until tomorrow . . . *mañana* . . . *mañana*. Yet, here was a boy who lived for something besides pleasure, a boy who had burned with an ideal, and had given his life for it.

There was a sudden commotion and I saw a middle-aged woman trying to break through the circle of soldiers. With a burst of superhuman strength she threw off the restraining hands and ran to the crumpled body and threw herself upon it, soaking herself in her son's blood. I turned away, sickened over man's inhumanity to man. I made my way to a taxi and rode out of the city and through the countryside toward the airport, but I could not shut out the memory of the hoarse sounds of that mother's grief, the eternal cry of a mother's pain.

The plane waited, silent and silvery, at the airport and I boarded it at once to slump in a back seat. We took off to climb the sky, higher and higher, until the entire island of Cuba was but the size of a stepping stone and then disappeared over the horizon of sea and sky. But the horrible image remained with me. I simply could not forget that crumpled young body, so frail, so easily broken by bullets. Yet the spirit in it, had the bullets destroyed it? I thought not. What is God's cannot be destroyed.

13

A Farewell and a Beginning

Las Vegas!

In the vastness of the desert there is a pinpoint of vivid, garish light that swells and glitters as the plane glides through the dusk from the distant mountain tops. As you come closer, ready to land, it stretches out to become aflame with neon tubes; the golden gulch, "The Strip," where each hotel tries to outshine its neighbor, where each is a lavish gambling casino.

Into these hotels are booked the entertainment industry's biggest stars, and at the highest prices in the world—yet, as Walter Winchell once remarked to me, "The stars are only shells for the game of chance."

The hotel lobbies are not conducive to the art of relaxation; they are filled with roulette wheels, they clatter with the sound of one-armed bandits, the click of dice,

and they hum with the almost audible silence surrounding
the "21" players. There are no clocks in the lobbies because the management doesn't want the customers to know
how late it is. Nor do the customers seeme to care, for
they seldom leave the tables before dawn—they often play
around the clock.

Crowding the gaming tables are ranchers in high boots,
gray-haired grandmothers with steel-rimmed spectacles,
mink-draped movie stars from Hollywood, vacationers
from Ohio, sophisticates from New York. But as they
stand shoulder to shoulder, all their differences drop away;
they are caught up in a common fever as their eyes are
hypnotized by the little white ball that spins 'round and
'round.

What is it that makes these people forget jobs, loves,
disappointments, responsibilities, to become creatures of
the wheel? I'm not certain, but it seems to me that gambling is a sort of concentrated simulation of life. As the
little ball spins around there is suspense and danger, yes,
and hope. When it finallys falls into a number, there is
triumph and elation, or bitter disappointment. And the
great advantage over real life is that you can relive the
entire gamut of emotions almost at once, at the next
spin of the wheel.

I have felt the lure of the tables; my game is called
"21," though it's always "22" to me. I face gloom or joy
on the turn of a card! Ah, but of course, my limit is
five dollars a game. And after I've lost a fair number of

these (and I always do), I fold up and quietly slip off the stool—giving the place to a braver (or more reckless) soul. Yes, I know what the gambling fever is and I respect it and fear it. I've felt the sick lure when money loses all value and you are simply tossing chips away.

Perhaps it was proper that my very last night-club appearance should be a return engagement at the fabulous Sahara Hotel. Certainly this was the top spot in club business. Nowhere did they present more lavish shows, nowhere brighter stars. While I was playing at the Sahara, or immediately following me, "The Strip" presented Jerry Lewis, Tony Martin, Pearl Bailey, Sammy Davis, Jr., Frank Sinatra, Marlene Dietrich, Liberace, and Elvis Presley.

The "Congo Room" at the Sahara is huge, with tables seating 1500 in mounting tiers around an elevated stage. It's not an intimate room, and you have to work "big" to make contact with the audience. Actually, Las Vegas audiences are not easy; they are so preoccupied with gambling that it's sometimes difficult to get them into a relaxed mood. Either they have won a lot and are, therefore, too excited to concentrate on you, or they have lost and are depressed and eager to get back to the tables and recoup.

Opening night was wonderful, however. The room seemed to be filled with winners and a happy buzz pervaded the scene. I was glad to know that here everybody could understand the language—but really it made no difference. We had a great time.

After the midnight show was over, I went out to the lobby and sat down on a stool at a "21" table. I had already learned the hard way that either I wasn't lucky or I just didn't know how to add up to 21. But I said to myself, "Oh well, just for a few games. After all, I had an exciting opening night and so maybe tonight is the lucky night." Ha! Famous last words. It wasn't that the losses upset me so much, but something else happened to me that made me spend long hours in some pretty serious soul-searching.

I was sitting at the gambling table with three other players and the dealer when it happened. Funny how you remember small details; I can remember exactly what kind of a hand I had. My two hole cards were an ace and a six, which meant I could count it as either seven or seventeen. I had been "hit" once and drew a ten, which meant I had to count the ace as one instead of eleven, otherwise I'd be over a total of twenty-one and out of the game. So there I sat with seventeen in my hand and pondering whether to draw again or to ride with it and hope the dealer would knock himself out. If I drew anything over a four I'd be ruined. The odds were against me, and yet I felt lucky, or maybe just reckless. I nodded to the dealer and he started to flip a card in front of me. Before he had finished, a voice shouted at me from behind, a voice that was both choked and strident with suppressed hysteria.

"Where is my daughter? You there, gambling, you,

Lillian Roth, what have you done with my daughter?"

The dealer looked past me with open mouth, my card still clutched in his hand, undealt. The other players turned and stared. At the roulette table next to us all the players and the croupier turned, forgetting for the moment the little white ball that filled the sudden silence with a thin whine as it raced unheeded around the edge of the wheel.

I swung around on my stool to find all eyes focused on a plump, motherly woman, dressed in her Sunday best. Her hands trembled as she clutched an imitation patent leather bag, and her neat straw hat was slightly askew.

"Where is my daughter?" she demanded again.

"I don't know what you're talking about," I said, and got off the stool to go to her. As I touched her shoulder she jerked away, her eyes blazing.

"You told her to run away from home," she cried. "You encouraged her!"

"Honestly, I don't know your daughter, I don't know what you're talking about." I saw the hotel detectives close about us but I motioned them to stay back.

The woman opened her purse and fumbled inside, finally pulling out two sheets of paper. On one was handwriting that was obviously mine, on the other a rather immature scrawl done in haste. I took the two papers and read them, my own first.

Then it came back to me, a correspondence I had had recently with a sixteen-year-old girl named Mary Ann

Mitchell, who lived in a nearby town. She was a stage-struck child and had begged advice concerning a career in the theater. I had been encouraging to her, I suppose, but certainly in a very general way, because I had no idea of her talents.

The second note was from Mary Ann. It read:

"Dear Mother and Father: I'm sorry to do this but I can't stand this terribly dull town and this terribly dull life any longer. The only thing I want in the whole world is to be an actress and I'll never be one as long as I stay here. Everybody here seems to laugh at me but I'm not like everybody else. I'm an actress and I know I'll have to suffer for my art. But I'm not afraid. I'm going to Holly-wood. I'll write you soon. I love you both and I'm sorry I have to do this but I do. Love, Mary Ann."

I returned the note to the distraught mother and said, "Please come with me."

As I had read the note, I remembered that just as I was about to go on stage for my midnight show, Burt had come backstage and said that a young girl was in the lobby and wanted to see me. He said she had hitchhiked here from her home town, was on her way to Hollywood but wanted to talk to me first. She had seemed quite up-set and he had taken her up to my room to wait for me until after the show.

Her presence upstairs had completely slipped my mind until this moment, but now I knew this must be Mary Ann. The mother would never believe that I didn't have

[*278*]

a hand in her daughter's disappearance, I was afraid. And, in truth, perhaps I did quite unknowingly. I had encouraged the girl but only as I would encourage anyone to try and create a life that was important and meaningful to him. But now the important thing was to reunite mother and daughter, to try and mend the family fabric.

As I led the mother to the elevator I tried to make her understand how I felt. But she cut me short, saying, "She's nothing but a child. She doesn't know her own mind."

"Perhaps that is true," I said, "but she *thinks* she does. And she's ambitious . . . and brave . . ."

"She's a minor," the mother snapped, "and she'll just have to understand that her father and I know what's best for her."

Did they know best, I wondered. Did Mary Ann know best? Did I? Did anybody know what was best for them in this world? We rode the elevator in silence.

When we entered my room, Burt was consoling Mary Ann. She was a thin child with delicate features and enormous black eyes that lit up at seeing me. Then she looked past me at her mother and an expression of betrayal swept over her. She cried, "You sent for her! You told her I was here!"

"No, Mary Ann. I didn't know you were here until just now so I couldn't have sent for her. Your mother just guessed it from our letters."

"Mary Ann . . ." her mother said in a firm voice.

The child shook her head and retreated a step. "You

can't make me go back," she cried. "Nobody can make me. I'm going to be an actress, no matter how much I have to suffer. You are old-fashioned—you don't understand."

She was being an actress at this moment, I thought. She was an adolescent fighting to grow, fighting for her independence, for her right to be an individual. And the mother was fighting for her baby. My heart went out to both of them. They were of each other's flesh, yet now they stood apart, hostile, angry, loving but rejected, and both so terribly alone in their anguish.

"Mary Ann . . ." the mother said, and there was a ragged edge to her voice. Suddenly she put her face in her hands and cried. Her shoulders shook and from between her fingers came gasping sobs, the sounds of her desolation.

I looked at Mary Ann and saw her eyes widen and then fill with tears. With a tiny cry of pain she ran to her mother and took her in her arms.

At last, when the tears were ended, I sat them down and we tried to talk it out. Each turned to me as arbiter, the mother appealing to my adult understanding of responsibility, the child appealing for support from the actress, the solidarity of one artist for another. Where was I to give my weight? I didn't know, I was no Solomon; I had no special wisdom. I was a woman who had made more than my share of mistakes, so why should they turn to me?

"There's one thing I'm sure of, Mary Ann," I said. "It was wrong of you to run away, to worry your mother.

Somehow, you should work this out with her and your dad."

"I've tried but she just won't listen to me. You tell her, make her understand how I've got to be an actress."

"I'm not sure I can," I said.

Mrs. Mitchell said, "I'm not a monster. I don't want to tie Mary Ann down. I want her to make something of her life but after all, she's only sixteen. She's too young to really know her mind and I want to try and protect her from taking a step that could ruin her life."

"Miss Roth," Mary Ann wailed, "tell her. Explain it to her."

"I think it's too late and everyone is too upset for explanations tonight. Please go home, Mary Ann, I promise to write you and your mother a long letter about how I feel. Okay?"

It was probably not one hundred percent okay with Mary Ann, but she accepted the proposition and mother and daughter left for home.

During the following days, I thought about Mary Ann and her problem a lot, because hers is like that of so many girls who have written me. What was I to say to her? To all of them? They expected pat answers and there just were none. Yet they deserved answers of some sort, serious and carefully thought-out answers. Well, I have done my best. Here is the letter I finally wrote to Mary Ann, and one which I now offer for what it is worth to all girls who "must become an actress" and to their harassed mothers.

Dear Mary Ann: I am writing to you from my hotel room. I've just completed the late show and it's past 2 A.M. I'm a little tired but I couldn't go to sleep until I tried to figure out something from my own experiences that might be of help to you and your mother.

In general, whenever anyone ends a phase of his life and looks at it in retrospect, as I am now doing, they ask themselves the question, "Would I want to relive my life? Knowing what I know now, would I follow the same career?" My answer to that is, Yes, I would. If I could live it knowing what I now know I could avoid quite a few pitfalls. But even if I could not, I am convinced that I would never have found any career as exciting and rewarding as mine, even with all its heartaches.

Looking at it from a different angle, from your mother's point of view: suppose *I* were a mother and had a talented daughter, would I want her to go into show business? Yes, I would if she desired it. I think my own mother was right when she encouraged me in the theater; she wanted me to have all the wonderful rewards that show business showers upon the talented. My mistakes, my unhappy marriages, my alcoholism, were not brought on by my theatrical career or my mother's hopes for me, they were a result of my own weaknesses. Show business is not responsible for the sin of self-destruction. Whether we stand or fall depends on our moral fiber, our intelligence, and our perseverance.

But please note, Mary Ann, that I said I'd want my

daughter in show business *if* she had *talent*. Not every-one has, you know, and all the wishing won't make a star. I don't know whether you have the ingredients or not, maybe you don't either, yet somehow you must be very sure you have them before you take the step. Circumstances can often make show business cruel; it can break the hearts of those who reach for the heavens but never leave the ground. I think this is what your mother is worried about, this is why she wants you to take your time, to be certain you're cut out for the theater.

You think your mother doesn't understand you. When you were here in my hotel room you kept appealing to me to explain things to her. Well, maybe she understands a lot more than you give her credit for. Do you realize that your Mom and I are about the same age? That sort of shocks you, doesn't it? Her hair is gray and there are some lines in her face, but did you ever stop to think they are badges of honor? Those lines are from worry over you, the gray hair from years of loving care, and from tears of both sorrow and happiness. I manage to keep my weight down because I have to for my business, and my hair looks light and bright because it's touched up. Your Mom is probably every bit as young in heart as I am; we just lead different kinds of lives and therefore look different. You can discuss your dreams with her. You may think that sometimes she's stubborn but I know one thing for cer-tain: she loves you as no one else does. Nobody will ever love you as your mother does.

Now let's assume for the moment that you do have talent. What then? The first thing is to realize that there's a long trip from the valley to the hilltop. And success isn't achieved by running away from home and "suffering" for your "art"; success comes from careful planning and long, hard work. Suffering is not reserved for artists alone.

Oh, yes, there have been a few youngsters who have hit it overnight, but rarely do they hold their position through the years. The only enduring success is that based upon hard work and the will to master your craft. There will be theatrical schools that will promise you quick and easy success (for a fee) but don't be taken in by them. Any legitimate school not only avoids promises, they go out of their way to tell you quite frankly that the road is rough.

At this point, Mary Ann, I can hear you saying to yourself, "I'm prepared for all the discouragements and heartaches, I'm prepared to suffer, because in the end it will all be worth it. Oh, the glamor and excitement of being a star, the exquisite clothes, the cool cars to ride in, the people clamoring after you . . ."

Ah, Mary Ann, after a time beautiful clothes become nothing more than dresses to cover you, the streamlined palaces on wheels are only transportation, and the crowds of admiring strangers that throng after you only serve to make you feel so terribly lonely when they are gone. But I don't suppose I can convince you of this, I don't suppose anyone can believe it until they've experienced it. From where you view things it does look glamorous, but I do know that all these material things do not constitute happiness.

If you become a star you'll face your problems in your own way. I want to talk not about the destination so much as the journey. Let's assume now that you've gone to a good school, you've learned the basic rudiments of your art and you're ready for your climb. In fiction, particularly in the movies, the young girl just starting out has a difficult time for a while but then is discovered by a big producer and the path is smoothed for her to stardom and probably matrimony with a rich man. But it's not likely to work out that way in real life, Mary Ann. In all probability you'll get a job, but then you'll have to use lots of strategy to keep your position.

Let's face it, there are a lot of people in show business, just as in any other business, who are worried and therefore aggressive and tricky. In night clubs there is a world of people who live apart from other people. Their upside-down existence lets them play and work when most people sleep, leading their lives in the harsh glare of electric lights, seldom warmed or soothed by the sun. And the king of this world is, as far as the performer is concerned, the night-club owner. Last year he may have been an insurance salesman or a stock broker, but suddenly he's the owner of a night club and that makes him an impressario. I've seen performers of forty years' standing booked into a club only to have their acts ripped apart by a club owner who had been in the business for less than a year.

But it's even tougher on the youngsters just starting out, as you will be, Mary Ann. These kids work to perfect a dance routine or a song or monologue, always hoping and believing that one night a big producer will catch their act and like it, only to have the club owner suddenly, at the last minute, tell them they are to have two minutes instead of fifteen, or that the show is long and they're cut entirely. There's real cruelty there. It's naked power, power in the cellar.

I'm not generalizing, of course, because there are some club owners who are very nice to performers. There is a Greek man who runs a pretty rough club in Colorado. It has a balcony for cheaper seats and the people up there are always setting up a ruckus and often throwing things down on the diners on the lower level. But they are generally quiet during the shows and it is one of the places I always liked to return to, primarily because the owner, with all his crudeness, watched out for me and kept his rough but lovable customers in line.

I remember once, when I was playing the Adolphus in Dallas, Texas, the manager did a very gracious thing. He knew I was a great picnic eater. As a matter of fact, when Burt and I were first married, I dragged him off to a lot of picnics. When we had the least money we'd get the greatest kick out of picnics, almost weekly loading up the car with goodies and heading into the countryside.

Often I'd say, "Burt, I'll get in the back seat with the

dogs. It will give more room for everybody." Of course, the picnic basket was in the back seat, too. We wouldn't have driven long before Burt would say, "What's the paper rattling for?"

"Oh, I guess it's the wind."

"Yeah, and that wind smells like roast beef."

I'd try to keep the paper quiet while I nibbled away at the picnic food. When we got to the spot where he intended to stop, the basket would be a shambles. Burt would look at it and shake his head. "I might have known."

"Well, the doggies got hungry," I'd alibi.

"Sure, and for the pickles and cole slaw too. They've got some palates."

But at this particular club, when I finished my last night and was getting into the car, there was an enormous basket in the back seat and on it a sign that read, "To a great lady." In it was an ice bucket, holding a foil-wrapped bottle. I thought, surely not champagne. But no, it was ginger ale. Other packages held gaily-wrapped sandwiches and gooey desserts. And roast beef bones for the dogs!

Then there was a man in a Western town from whom I will ever have a soft spot in my heart. He was the first man to pay me $4,000 a week. He owned one restaurant in town and had just bought out a club that had featured strip-tease and he was trying to convert it into a smart supper club. Not with too much success, either. When I arrived, I found the place looked like a gloomy beer parlor, with dark booths around the edge of the room, and a bare wooden stage at one end. Moreover, the newspaper in town was owned by a man who was opposed to liquor and so he refused to take any advertising from the night spots selling it.

On the first night, the customers were rather confused about my act. Many didn't know there had been a change of policy, and kept yelling for me to "take it off." I'm afraid my non-strip act fell pretty flat.

On a Sunday night, there were only three or four tables occupied, maybe ten people in the whole place. I went to the owner just before show time and said, "Look, there's only a handful of people here, and I kind of feel out of place anyway, so if you want to cancel my contract and save the money, it's all right with me."

"No, Lillian," he said, "you go on. You're not singing to them, you're singing to me. I love to listen to you. It's worth the money. Go on, Lillian, and sing for me."

I did, with all my heart.

So you see, Mary Ann, there are good people to make up for the hurts in the night-club business. But the hard men seem to turn up when you're weak and vulnerable. So, remember these slaps when you are making your decisions. Can you take it?

You've no doubt read about stars being interviewed by the press and thought to yourself how exciting it must be to have every word you say eagerly listened to and reported. Well, yes and no, Mary Ann. Of course, if the press suddenly loses interest in you, that can only mean you're no longer a star, of no interest to the newspaper and magazine readers, and that is something you try to avoid. For without the press your efforts are without voice.

No matter how tired you may be, or what your personal problems, you have to receive the press pretty much at their convenience because they have deadlines to make. And better be at your best. If a reporter sees crowsfeet around your eyes or a slump of fatigue to your shoulders, he's apt to report it and then the readers will think, "Well, I guess she's had it."

And if the reporters probe tender spots, as they often do, you would do well to conceal the pain because they may magnify it. You try always to answer reporters' questions honestly, because they'll soon have you spotted as a phony if you don't, but you've got to be careful in your answers, use temperate words, because any emotional outburst seems to sound twice as violent in print as you intended it when you spoke.

I guess what I'm trying to tell you is that you will have no privacy, that there will be no dark corners you can crawl into when you're hurt or frightened, no way of nursing your wounds in secret. As long as you're a star, your life is legitimate material for the press.

Actually, I have been fortunate in my relations with the men and women of the press. I have been honest with them and they have been generally fair with me, more than fair—they have encouraged me and given me a boost when I needed it most.

There have been times when I received bad reviews, of course, and they hurt. An actor tends to forget all the good notices and remember the cutting one. I recall when I was sixteen years old, I played Texas Guinan's club in New York (my, that was way back in 1926!) and the audience was wonderful to me, in fact, I practically stopped the show. All the critics raved about me, except one. George Jean Nathan wrote a review in the *New Yorker* in which he said, ". . . The audience must have been packed with her relatives." I was terribly hurt and shaken. Nathan had a magazine to attack me, I had nothing with which to answer.

Some time later, I read an article by George Bernard Shaw in which he attacked Nathan, saying that a man who uses words like "garbage pail" to describe the work of serious artists doesn't deserve to be a critic, that he makes no contribution to the theater. It went on for four scathing pages. I clipped it and sent it to Nathan, along with a little note which said, "You had your right to your opinion of me, even if it hurt. But I guess I came out ahead because I only had one sentence to worry about, while you've got four pages!"

There is one female columnist in New York who has always gone out of her way to write cutting things about me. I don't know why, maybe she's resentful of me in some obscure way that even she doesn't understand, but I can always count on her to have the knife out for me. One time when I came to New York she wrote that I had "sneaked into town to avoid process servers," when the truth was I was there to appear on Ed Sullivan's television show where any process server, and millions of other people, could see me.

At another time, just before my picture came out, she wrote, "Lillian Roth is so mad at the motion picture industry for not letting her sing in *I'll Cry Tomorrow* that she goes on stage and does an imitation ridiculing Susan Hayward imitating her. It may panic Lillian Roth, but not the audience." I was shocked at that one. In the past I had never bothered to try to correct anything she said. I just figured that it would add fuel to the fire. But this time I wrote and told her that I was doing a satire on myself singing "Red, Red Robin" the way I introduced it when I was sixteen, and it had nothing to do with Susan, even though she sang it in the picture. I wrote, "I hope you'll correct this because Susan was my choice for the part in the picture and why would I want to hurt her? If you saw my act you should have realized I was only kidding my old style and I hope you'll make this clear in your next column." Of course, she never did.

I haven't even mentioned the dregs of journalism that feed like vultures on the life's blood of the profession. I mean those sensational, "inside dope" magazines that disgrace our newsstands. I dislike even mentioning them to you, but they are part of the picture, part of the world of show business you are so eager to enter. These magazines go beyond all bounds of decency. They destroy reputations, careers, lives, for no reason except to pander to the ghoulish appetites of diseased minds. I knew an actress in Hollywood who had given up her career and was happily married and the mother of two wonderful children when one of these magazines did a job on her, printed a story about the love affairs she had had years and years before she was married. Her husband left her, her children were shocked, hurt, and cut adrift, and the woman went to pieces and wound up in a sanatorium. To dare to come out after eight or ten years with a story about her past lovers, even if it was true, was terribly cruel. If God can forgive you, if the priest or minister can say to you, "Go and sin no more," then who are these ghouls who dare to malign, disinter, and destroy?

One of these magazines tried to do a job on me a few years ago. The headline on the cover carried this challenge: "Lillian Roth, Sue Us If You Dare!" I don't know how many people bought that magazine to read an exposé of my sins, but they were let down. All that was inside were uncredited excerpts from my own book. I had told all there was to be told about Lillian Roth and there was nothing new the scandalmongers could dig up. Of course, they twisted the facts; they said I had killed my mother, ruined my dad and my husbands. But that was pure malice and hate and there was little I could do about it except cry inside.

All of which adds up to this, Mary Ann: In show business you have no such thing as a personal life. If you make mistakes, the public will sooner or later hear about them. The spotlight is on you, not only while you're on stage, but off stage as well. And some people's nerves can't take this constant surveillance.

Think of your own life, Mary Ann. You're young and I'm sure you haven't done anything too bad, but think back and see if you wouldn't be upset if *everything* you'd done thus far was suddenly printed for the whole world to read. All right, that's what you'll have to face for the rest of your life if you go into show business. It's really a glass house. Can you be happy under these conditions? I don't know. You'll have to answer that question for yourself.

This letter is longer than I intended, goodness knows, but advising someone on a life's career is a very awesome responsibility, something not to be done lightly or briefly. I think that by now I have made most of the points I had in mind, except perhaps one—money.

Oh, I know that the big money in show business is a great lure to you, Mary Ann, and there is no reason why you shouldn't want it. We all like pretty clothes and nice homes and financial security. But I can't close without saying a few words of warning about that money. It can be a problem, even an evil, if you're not careful.

You told me that you had read my book *I'll Cry Tomorrow*, so I know that you understand how poorly I handled my money the first time I was making it. With

God's help I'll never repeat those mistakes, but that doesn't mean I don't still find it a problem. Let me try and explain.

When you have a lot of money, more than you need for your own wants and for old-age security, what are you going to do with it? Give it away? Oh, that sounds easy, even exciting. You can imagine all sorts of needy people and causes you could help with your largess, but it doesn't always work that way.

There is a very human tendency to give money in order to win approval or fame or even to purchase influence in an organization or in someone's life. This can be disastrous to the giver's peace of mind because those things should never be for sale.

I must say that the giving of little gifts unexpectedly and with no strings attached can be a lot of fun. I remember recently, when I appeared on a television show on the West Coast, the sponsor gave me a 21-inch TV set. Now, I already had three television sets, and a half-dozen radios, and certainly I did not need a new one. The only thing to do was to give it away. But to whom?

I thought of a friend of mine, but I knew she wouldn't keep the set for her own pleasure but would pass it along to her niece. I thought I might send it to a religious order, or an old people's home, or a veterans' hospital, but I had the feeling it was destined for a *person*, not an institution. I guess I wanted actually to see the pleasure it could afford someone. But who?

When it came time for us to leave on a tour, there was the TV set still undisposed of. "Burt," I said, "you'll have to put the TV set in the trailer."

"Oh no!" he wailed. "Not that! Do you know how much stuff we have to put in that trailer?"

"I don't care. Someone is waiting for this set and I'm not going to leave it behind."

Poor, patient Burt found a spot for it and off we went on our tour. The first club was in Phoenix and when we arrived I found the club had hired a Negro maid for me. She was the cutest thing—all two hundred fifty pounds of her looked like Aunt Jemima, with a beautiful smile, and a chuckle that started way down deep. My dressing room was a trailer parked just outside the club's kitchen entrance, and every night when this gal came in to help me dress for the show—well, we both threatened to squeeze right back out the door like a squirt of toothpaste. She was a grand person, though, and one night I got her to talk about herself.

"My husband walked out on me a couple of years ago, just walked out and left me and the three children."

"Oh, how dreadful," I said.

"Well, I guess so. But it ain't the end of the world. Nothin's really the end of the world. I just went to work, that's all. I don't believe in going down and getting unemployment money, like a lot of folks. Not while I'm healthy. I got pride, I guess. I gotta have a job and support myself and my children and there ain't no two ways about that. I got a good mother who lives next door to me and I was brought up to be honest and that's the way I try to be."

"But it must be hard for you sometimes," I said.

She shrugged her massive shoulders. "We make out." Then she giggled. "I just got one special prayer I give up to the good Lord from time to time. I tell Him there's only two luxury things I want, a washing machine for myself, and a television set for my children."

"Honey," I said, "you got half your prayer answered. There's a TV set for you in the back of the car."

When she came to work the next evening she was just bubbling over with happiness. "Miss Roth," she cried, "you should have seen them three babies of mine when I left 'em. I tucked 'em into bed and then put the television up on the dresser at the foot of the bed. There was six of the biggest, roundest eyes you ever did see in your life."

So you see, Mary Ann, it can be a joy to give things away, but you have to work at it. It's not easy to do it properly, you must always be sure you give from the heart and not make the receiver beholden.

If you become a star, Mary Ann, and certainly if you enter show business I hope you do, there is one thing you must remember above all else—you didn't accomplish it alone. Your drama and voice teachers, the writers of your material, the electricians and sound men, the musicians, the ushers, the waiters, the set designers, the wardrobe mistresses, script girls, and business managers . . . they all had a hand in your success. They each fit a piece of themselves into the mold that made the star. If you do forget them, if you cut them off from your life after you've hit the top, you'll be a very lonely girl and a very remorseful one.

I know a certain famous comedian who had members of his family on his staff all the time he was struggling to get to the top. One brother was his business manager, another publicity manager, a sister was costume designer and wardrobe mistress for his big TV shows. All these were skilled in their various jobs and contributed mightily to the comedian's success. Yet when he thought he had it made, when he thought he was so big that he could just coast, he began to resent his relatives, began to think they were leeches who just sponged on his talent. And he fired them all.

From that moment on, he began to go downhill in his profession. The quality of his work changed, his great ego and his selfishness began to come through to the audience. They stopped tuning in his television shows and pretty soon the sponsor cancelled, and the great man was out of work. He thought he had made his success alone, but in truth, he had only made his failure alone.

A final bit of advice, Mary Ann. Analyze your own temperament very carefully before you make the plunge into show business. If you are the type of person who longs for emotional tranquillity, then this career is not for you. There is no serenity in show business, its place is taken by ambition, work, nerve-wracking hours, and the unslakable thirst always to do better and better. I'm not saying you can never have peace of mind, because you can. But it comes from work and achievements, from the realization of a hard day's job well done.

When you are in show business, serenity of spirit can only be achieved on a separate level. You can have a spirituality, an in-tuneness with God, but that is apart from your life and your career on earth.

I hope all this has been a help to you and your mother. My very best to you, Mary Ann, in whatever decision you make.

Happy tomorrows,
Lillian Roth

It was dawn when I finally put down my pen. I pulled off the covers and slid into bed. But sleep wouldn't come. I was exhausted, but in spirit more than in body. A deep depression settled over me. While I had been writing of my career, trying to distill some advice out of it for Mary Ann, I had felt strong and alive. It had seemed to me an appropriate way to end a phase of my life. Yet now I felt weak and empty.

With only two night-club performances ahead of me before the final curtain fell, I was suddenly full of indecision. Was I making a big mistake? Was I wrecking my career? For almost forty years I had been singing songs for audiences, and to end it was like losing part of me. Now that the moment had come, I was afraid.

I was doing what I wanted to do. I was doing what was right, I *knew* I was, but still I was afraid. I could give advice to a young girl, yet I had difficulty taking it myself. I felt ashamed of my weakness. Sleep was out of the question. I got up and dressed and walked out of the hotel to get a taxi and head for town.

As we rode along the deserted streets, I saw a sexton opening the front doors of a church. I stopped the cab and entered the church, dropping down in a back row among the vast shadows. I sat there quietly. I didn't intend to ask God to show me what to do, I *knew* what I had to do; I did not even want to ask Him for strength, for I had it within me and it was my responsibility to summon it up. No, I only wanted to be in the house of the Lord for a while, to savor His peace and tranquillity.

That evening, I gave the last two performances of my life as a night-club entertainer. A thousand faces swirled around me, laughing, admiring, wishing me luck. Would I ever again be the center of such attention? Would I ever again hear applause roll up from the audience . . . just for me?

Perhaps not, but I had made my decision.

14

Coming Home

I never had a real home until I was forty-six years old. I had been married four times, but never had a lawn to mow, a rose bush to tend, or a back porch to sit on and watch the sunset.

When my sister and I were children in vaudeville, we used to sit by the train window during the long, lonely rides between towns and gaze at other children's houses. I can still remember the haunting sadness that filled us as the train would sweep past back yards full of playing children with the fathers and mothers sitting on the porches, relaxed, content, waiting for darkness and sleep. I told myself that one day soon I'd have a home, too, and all the love and security that went with it.

Instead, I lived my life in hotel rooms or apartments, and no matter how I might try to decorate them, they never quite seemed to belong to me; I had no roots in them, I could move out the next day for a different apartment without any feeling of loss.

How strange always to have wanted something so badly and never have it. The smallest wage earners seemed to manage homes; I had made a million dollars in my lifetime, and I had never been able to have one.

But now things were going to be different. After all these years I was to be like other women. I walked out of the Sahara Hotel in Las Vegas on the last Monday in April, climbed into the car beside Burt, and headed south and west toward our new home in Palm Springs.

Burt and I had previously owned a house in Fort Lauderdale for a few years and I adored it, but somehow it wasn't a home because I was never in it for more than one or two weeks out of the year, when I happened to be working clubs in Miami. No, Palm Springs would be my first real home because I was going to live there. I'd have a garden and put in seeds and still be there when the seeds began to push up through the earth; still be there when they turned magically into flowers; and still be there when the flowers faded and fell in life's cycle.

Burt and I had spotted our "dream house" in Palm Springs about six months before. I had been there to appear at the Chi Chi Club and the desert captured me. There was a haunting beauty I had found in no other place. A spirituality, too. When I first saw the desert I had the strangest feeling that I had been there before, maybe years ago, or even centuries. Yesterday and today seemed to telescope into one with the desert's eternalness. The French philosopher Lecomte du Noüy wrote that in centuries to come "all men will revert to the desert" in order to find the absolute spiritual truths.

I suppose that in 1957 I was rushing the migration a bit, but I knew the desert would be a fine tonic for me after the years in smoke-filled night clubs. To wake up in the morning, look out my bedroom window, and see the same patch of God's earth I had seen the morning before; to know the exact spot on a mountain peak where the sun would rise; to know the shifting, brooding moods of nature, not in a thousand different places, but in one! That was what a home meant to me.

When I was playing the Chi Chi Club in November 1956, I had said to Burt, "This is where I belong. This is home."

"It's a wilderness," he observed.

All my life I'd lived in a wilderness of loneliness, but this was nature, and nourishing. I tried to explain it to Burt.

He thought about it a moment, then said, "Maybe this is right for you, Lillian. You can have your solitude in the desert, yet it's only twenty minutes by air from Holly-wood. If we got your dramatic career rolling you should be close to Hollywood."

"Of course," I said, though I must confess that I hadn't thought about the career aspects of living in Palm Springs.

That was Burt's job. "Let's start building a house right away," I cried.

"Lillian," he laughed, "you always want everything done yesterday. It takes time to find land and then have an architect draw plans and finally have a builder go to work."

"Maybe we could find one already built that would suit us," I said.

"Maybe. I'll get in touch with a real estate agent this afternoon."

Graham Dexter, an Englishman with a love of our land, helped us find a house on the edge of town. It wasn't exactly right for our needs (I wanted a house with twenty closets with rooms attached), but Burt began to explain to me how we could remodel it. As we walked through the rooms and around the grounds, a vision of the remodeled house began to form in our minds. One wing would have my bedroom, Burt's bedroom, and a third room that could be an office, along with two baths. In the center of the house we imagined a sweeping living-dining room, and in the other wing a kitchen, servants' rooms, a library, and a guest room with bath. And the entire front of the house would have eaves-to-ground glass walls, looking out on the terrace and the swimming pool.

The pool was already in existence and around it was a patio landscaped with shrubs, palm trees, and flowering bushes. Behind it all towered the awe-inspiring backdrop of the San Jacinto Mountains. And now, as we looked, the sun went down behind these craggy mountains and they turned from brown to a brooding purple and finally to black.

"Well, Lillian," Burt said, "what do you think?"

"Oh yes, this it it. This is where I want to live the rest of my life. That is, if you like it."

"I like it fine."

"Then let's get an architect and a builder and have it remodeled just the way you explained it. Let's have it all ready to move into the week I finish night life . . . the good Lord willing."

And so it was to be.

Everything had been purchased, hired, engaged, paid for, and the house was now to be ready to receive us. The pool maintenance men were to have the pool cleaned and filled; the air-conditioning engineers were to have followed the carpenters and plasterers; the painters were to have followed the air conditioners; and the interior decorator was to have climaxed it all. I told the decorator I wanted my room done in royal blue, with lipstick red pillows, and the rest of the house in black and white. There were to be lots of mirrors on walls to catch and reflect the pool and the mountains behind it.

Six months had passed. Now there remained but a mere two hundred miles and we'd be home. Forty-six years and how many thousands of night clubs had added up to this moment? I couldn't calculate it all, but it was going to be worth it.

Our car's engine sang a full-throated song of power as we climbed through the mountains . . . we're going home . . . we're going home . . . we're going home. Then a narrow, craggy pass opened, we roared through it and there, spread before us, was the ageless desert. And at its far rim, nestled against the base of the San Jacinto Mountains, was Palm Springs—home.

As we raced across the floor of the desert we were pursued by an unusual cold, rain-filled wind, and black clouds glowered from above. No matter, soon we would be home and protected. In my mind's eye I could see the living room aglow with warm lights, the draperies pulled against the gathering gloom outside.

The house and grounds were surrounded by a high fence. We pulled up before the gate and I jumped out of the car, followed by my barking, excited dogs. I threw open the gate and stepped into the yard—and devastation. The lawn was buried under discarded piles of building materials, the flower beds were untended, the palm trees were drooping and dejected from lack of care, and the swimming pool! I cried out, "Who's drowning?" But, no, it was only a raft of discarded lumber and insulation. The green pool was black, apparently having been mistaken for a cesspool and disposal unit. Ah, but the house, I thought, surely that would be ready for me.

I slid open the door and stepped into—a shambles! The white floor was black with heedless feet.

"Oh, my floor!" I wailed.

Burt said, "Nice pattern. Black on white looks lovely."
He cringed under my glare.

Packing boxes cluttered most of the space, a few pieces
of furniture were piled in a corner. Workmen's tools were
scattered about. A white leather chair held two pairs of
overalls; a Roman statue was wearing a painter's cap; a
Grecian bronze lady, in a pose similar to our Statue of
Liberty, held not a light aloft but in the upturned palm
of her hand a dead cigar. Ropes, mops, buckets, brooms,
ladders, nails, tin cans, paint brushes, putty, wires . . .
that was the decor!

And then came the invasion of the workmen. I spread
my feet and put my hands on my hips and demanded an
accounting. They had had six months to finish the place.
Why was it a shambles? Maybe the answers made sense,
but not to me.

Pool maintenance man: "I tried to clean the pool but
the gardener just kept letting the dirt drift into it."

Gardener: "I tried to fix the garden but the workmen
were walking over it all the time, pulling supplies, up-
rooting everything I planted. What was I to do?"

Floor covering man: "Look, lady, I know the tiles
shouldn't be down until all the painting is through, but it
never got through. You want a floor to walk on, don't
you?"

Painter: "No use painting the final coat until all the
wall switches and plugs are in. Only have to do it over
again."

[*309*]

Electrician: "I'm only a sub-contractor, lady. I can't put in the switches until the plastering is done. It's not my fault things aren't ready."

Interior decorator: "Oh my dear, you'll never know what I've been through, what trouble I've had with that contractor. Really!"

Finally, I just gave up and went into my room, closed the door and sat on a packing box and wept.

Over the following weeks I was to learn the truth of something observed by Ralph Waldo Emerson: "A man builds a fine house; and now he has a master, and a task for life; he is to furnish, watch, show it, and keep it in repair the rest of his days."

Oh, the time and energy required to run a house. This is nothing new to housewives throughout the world, but it was new to me, and thrilling, too. I didn't begrudge a minute spent in hanging drapes or planning the garden, or scrubbing the floor, because now it was for real and forever. And now the rewards of having a home began to come. I began to feel rooted to a piece of God's good earth, I had a sense of belonging. When it rained I saw it wash and freshen *my* house and *my* garden; when God sent the sun, it was to warm and nourish *my* flowers . . . and His.

The big patio was there for my three dogs. I loved these helpless little animals with all my heart and I knew how difficult it had been for them to be constantly traveling and cramped up in hotels and never, for months on end, being able to smell the delicious odor of growing things.

Bambi is the oldest, a ten-year-old chihuahua. Her real name is Conchita Louisa Maria, but for a dog that weighs only three pounds that seemed a pretty heavy load. Because she resembled Walt Disney's Bambi, that became her nickname. Then there is two-year-old Do-do, a toy French poodle we acquired at Las Vegas at a time when the doctors had given Bambi up. Burt, not wanting me to brood too much in case of Bambi's death, suddenly appeared with this ball of white, kinky wool. I said, "Oh no, Bambi will get worse if she has another dog around to share our love. We can't do this." But Bambi got better, and I think because Do-do loved her from the first.

The trio is completed by our Pomeranian named Butch, who looks more like a white fox fur. Butch got the name because, though female and small in size, she's big in heart and courage and enthusiasm. Every morning she looks at me with an expression that says, "Well, what's new? What's doing? Let's see what mischief we can stir up today."

Bambi, on the other hand, is neurotic and unsure of herself, which tends to make her snappy. They say that animals take on human characteristics after they have lived with humans for a while. Well, Bambi has lived with me for ten years so I guess that explains that. The poor little thing took on my past idiosyncrasies.

Now these three dogs had a home for the first time, had

their own patch of yard, their own trees, their own hearth to warm, their own big establishment to protect from trespassers. How they loved it!

My very first house guest was my old and dear friend, Rosalind Berle, Milton's sister. "House guest"—what wonderful words! I could never have had a "house guest" when I lived in hotels and motels, or even in an apartment. For a "house" guest you need a "house," and now I had one. So there!

One afternoon, Roz and I were splashing in the pool when she said, "Lilly, when Burt comes back from town let's have him take a snapshot of us."

"Okay," I said.

"Don't you remember the last one we had taken together in bathing suits? At Manhattan Beach!"

"When we were ten years old!" I cried. "I've had one of those snaps around for years. Remember the long-drawer bathing suits down over our knees? Did we think we were hot stuff! Or should we say—cool? What was the term we used then? Oh, I remember—the cat's meow!"

We got to reminiscing about the old days when the Roths and the Berles were neighbors and good friends. Roz's mother and mine, Sandra and Katie, were devoted to each other even though they were in a competitive situation.

I said, "Gee, I can remember your mother calling up and saying, 'My Milton said the funniest thing today. He had everyone in stitches.'"

"Sure . . . sure," Roz said, "and I can remember Katie calling all the time and saying, 'You must come over and hear my Lilly sing Madame Butterfly in Italian.'"

I laughed. "Here we are, together just like our mothers were. History repeating itself."

Roz said, "And remember how they used to love to play cards? By the hour! Gosh!"

I remembered. And when times were rough for my poor mother, when every cent she had went to trying to pull me out of my alcoholism, she couldn't afford the low-stake poker games she loved so dearly and Sandra Berle used to say to her, "Come, take my hand and sit in for me for a while."

Mother was always very proud and would refuse, but she'd explain later, "What fun is there in winning or losing for somebody else? No, it's got to be your own money." It was a matter of principle with her, and she would never give in.

Roz and I fell silent, floating in the water and looking up at the great arch of heaven with a sudden feeling of awe. Both our mothers were dead and, I was convinced, united in that heaven. And if playing cards together had been one of their happiest pleasures on earth, surely there must be some heavenly equivalent for them. They must feel great pleasure, too, in knowing that Roz and I were together after all these years, that their two girls still loved each other and were continuing the relationship first set by Katie and Sandra.

Yes, a house is for a house guest, and especially one who is an old and dear friend.

One afternoon, I was in the study reading play manuscripts when there came a knock at the front gate, followed by the entrance of a girl I had known in the clubs back East. She was in Palm Springs for an engagement and had decided to look me up, for old times' sake. I was delighted to see her and we shop-talked, catching up on what mutual friends were doing. But every now and then I caught her looking at me with a puzzled, searching expression. At last she came out with what was on her mind.

"Lillian," she said, "what's this I hear about you giving up club work?"

"It's true," I said. "I'm going to be a serious actress, or else . . ."

"Honey, serious actresses aren't always working."

"I know."

"I don't want to seem nosey, but what were you making in the clubs?"

"About ten thousand dollars a week."

She shook her head in bewilderment. "You gave up ten thousand dollars a week just for a dream. Lillian, you must be crazy."

I laughed, "Don't worry, I won't starve. I've got a few dollars saved for my old age."

"But to give all that up! What do we work for but money?"

"Oh, come now!" I exclaimed. "Lots of things."

"Well, a few others . . . excitement, success, glamor, and admiration. But you're giving up all that too. You're going to start over at the bottom, honey. You're going to be knocking on agents' doors month after month. You'll give readings of parts and be told you're not the type. You'll finally get parts and go through the long agony of rehearsals only to have the show close somewhere in the sticks. Or you'll open on Broadway to have the critics sneer, and the show play five performances. This sort of heartache is all right for the kids, Lillian, but we're too old for it. It can break our hearts. You've got it made in the clubs, stay where it's warm and safe."

"Warm and safe," I mused. "It's not enough."

She threw up her hands in despair. "Well, it sure is for me, I can tell you."

I could see she didn't understand what I was trying to say and we turned to other subjects, but after she had gone I thought about the conversation, and about the question she had raised.

It was enough for her to be warm and safe, she had said. But the truth was, there is no warmth and safety in this life. In the next one, yes, but not in this one. For us, now, life is a constant struggle and to stop struggling is to stop living. We may weary of it, we may denounce it, but if we are to live and grow we cannot avoid it.

And that struggle is not for money! At least, not for money alone. We struggle to realize the best that is within

[*315*]

us—spiritually, physically, morally, artistically, in short, we struggle to create our best selves. And in this way we draw close to God.

He gave us our talents and by utilizing them to the utmost we follow His plan for us. To do this is to achieve peace of mind, almost a state of grace; failure to do this leaves us with a troubled conscience, an empty, rasping, out-of-tune life that offers no rewards of any real value. These truths apply equally to me, trying to be a good actress, as to the stone mason trying to build a true, sound wall.

How often have we seen a man with all the appearances of success, money, and position, yet about him is an aura of bitterness, a sourness of soul? However much money this man had made, he was not a success in his heart because he had not made the most of himself. He felt cheated by life and he didn't realize he had only himself to blame.

And on the other hand, haven't you often seen a man in modest circumstances, perhaps a gardener or a filling-station attendant, who had a sunny disposition and seemed at peace with the world? Those were men who may have had limited capabilities but were using them to full capacity. They were getting the most out of life and they knew it.

Looking back over the years, I see evidence of this on every side. Jean Thoney, strapped to a wheel chair, could smile at the world because she had been able to accept God's pattern for her. Eugene Logan, sentenced to prison for life, knew peace of mind because he was making the most of his God-given talents. Whatever his past sins, he is now closer to God than those men who are lazy and disrespectful of their talents. None of us can escape responsibility to God for the use of the talents He gave us.

And so it is that I, at forty-six years of age, am now trying to clear my life of the accumulated clutter of the past, both the failures and the triumphs, because I *must* go on to the full utilization of my talents. And it has nothing to do with money, one way or the other. Twenty dollars a week or ten thousand, that is not God's measure of our accomplishments, and therefore it is never really ours, either. We often go to elaborate lengths to fool ourselves, but we never really succeed. In our hearts and in our souls we know when we cheat.

If there is one thought I hold closest, it is the knowledge that we never walk alone. We have but to look up and truthfully say, "Lord, I am doing my very best." He then gives us the serenity we all so desperately need.

You try it and see.